RAPID REVISION NOTES
O LEVEL

ENGLISH LANGUAGE BOOK 2

by
D.C. Perkins

CELTIC REVISION AIDS

CELTIC REVISION AIDS
Lincoln Way, Windmill Road,
Sunbury on Thames, Middlesex

© C.E.S. Ltd.

First published 1980

ISBN 0 17 751252 0

Printed in Hong Kong

CONTENTS

SERIES INTRODUCTION

Celtic Revision Aids Rapid Revision Notes are designed for use by students studying for CSE or 'O' level examinations.

The syllabus content has been divided into a number of fairly short and self-contained sections. For each section, the facts relating to that part of the syllabus are given as a series of easy-to-follow notes. Examples are given as appropriate and the section is concluded by giving a number of practice examination questions. Where these questions involve numerical work the correct answers are given at the end of the book.

The book is rounded off by a section on examination technique and you are strongly recommended to read these suggestions carefully.

These Rapid Revision Notes should be used to remind you of the essential facts of the subject as you prepare for the examination. Further practice in examination technique and familiarity with actual examination questions can be gained by using the Celtic Revision Aids Model Answers 'O' level and Multiple Choice 'O' level books for this subject.

AUTHOR'S PREFACE

This book is one of a series of books designed for students revising for G.C.E. 'O' Level, C.S.E. and 16+. It is a comprehensive revision aid which can be used on its own, with other books in the series or to complement a formal course of instruction in the subject. Students studying at home, those using correspondence lessons and those in school or further education will find it especially useful because it is organised to facilitate recall and pin-point areas of difficulty.

Where the exercises form an integral part of the explanation of work they are answered in the text. Additional exercises embodied in the text are answered in a key at the end of the volume.

ESSENTIAL SPELLING

Many people have trouble with their spelling. However, spelling is not too difficult if you remember simple rules. The following should help you.

1. In general, remember words are spelt as they sound. Thus, always listen carefully to how a word is pronounced for this often gives a clue to how it is spelt.

2. Read as much English as possible and take note of words that are new to you.

3. Refer to a dictionary as often as possible. Keep it by your side — constant reference will fix the meanings and the spellings in your mind.

4. Learn to recognise the most common prefixes and suffixes. These will help your spelling. (See Rapid Revision English Book I.)

5. English has borrowed and adopted words from other languages. An awareness of this will help your spelling. (An etymological dictionary is often helpful.)

Below are a number of simple spelling rules. A knowledge of these will enable you to spell large groups of words correctly. It is unfortunate that some spelling rules are so complicated — or have so many exceptions — that they are only confusing. The following are some of the less involved rules followed by lists of irregular plurals and difficult plurals which should be committed to memory.

SPELLING RULES

1. **The problem of doubling.** This is when to double a letter and when not to double.

   (i) When a monosyllabic word ends in a single consonant preceded by a single vowel the last letter is doubled, e.g.,

   | hit | — | hitting |
   | bat | — | batting |

(ii) When a word ends with one 'l' this is doubled when there is a vowel ending, e.g.,

travel	—	travelling

(iii) When a word ends with one 'l' retain this 'l' when the suffix 'ly' is added, e.g.,

final	—	finally
cool	—	coolly
full	—	fully

(iv) When the prefixes 'im', 'ir' or 'un' are added to a word double the 'm', 'n' or 'r', e.g.,

responsible	—	irresponsible
reputable	—	irreputable
revocable	—	irrevocable
natural	—	unnatural

(v) When the prefix 'dis' is added to a word with an initial 's' doubling occurs, e.g.,

satisfied	—	dissatisfied

(vi) Generally a letter is not doubled if the final consonant is preceded by two vowels, e.g.,

wear	—	wearing
fear	—	fearing

2. **The problem of 'ie' and 'ei'.** The rule that everyone learns is — 'use i before e except after c'.

(i) When the first syllable has the sound of 'a' as in neighbour or weigh use 'e' before 'i', e.g.,

> freight;   vein;   rein;   deign.

(ii) When the word has the sound of 'ee' as in steed or deer use 'i' before 'e' except after 'c', e.g.,

achieve pier	—	'i' before 'e'
receipt deceit	—	'e' before 'i' after 'c'

NOTE the following exceptions — weird; either; neither; seize and leisure.

(iii) Note that many words do not fit any rule and have to be learned, e.g.,

> friend; sieve; foreign; mischief and sovereign.

3. The problem of the final 'y'.

(i) The final 'y' of a word changes to 'i' before any ending except '—ing' if it is preceded by a consonant, e.g.,

dry	—	drying
buy	—	buying
happy	—	happiness

(ii) The final 'y' is changed to 'i' when the 'y' is preceded by a consonant and other letters are added, e.g.,

beauty	—	beautiful
lady	—	ladies

(iii) The final 'y' remains unchanged before any ending, if it is preceded by a vowel, e.g.,

stay	—	staying
play	—	playing
pay	—	payment

4. The problem of the 'e' ending, that is, whether to drop it, e.g.,

> blame   —   blamable

(i) Drop the 'e' before a vowel suffix, e.g.,

> love   —   lovable

(ii) Return the 'e' before a consonant or when the 'e' softens a 'c' or 'g' ending, e.g.,

love	—	lovely
advantage	—	advantageous

5. The problem of silent letters. Many words in English have silent letters. Some of these are knuckle; lamb; psalm; campaign; write and whistle. These have to be learnt.

6. **The problem of forming plurals.**

(i) Generally, the plural of nouns in English is formed by adding 's', e.g.,

| girl | — | girls |
| boy | — | boys |

(ii) The plural is formed by adding 'es' when it is difficult to pronounce, e.g.,

| church | — | churches |
| bus | — | busses |

(iii) Words ending in a consonant and 'y' change the 'y' to 'i' before adding 'es' to the plural, e.g.,

| lady | — | ladies |
| party | — | parties |

(iv) Words ending in a vowel and 'y' add 's' to the plural only, e.g.,

| day | — | days |

(v) Many words ending in 'f' or 'fe' change to 'ves' in the plural. However, many simply add 's'.

(vi) Words ending in 'ff' always add 's' to the plural, e.g.,

| cuff | — | cuffs |
| cliff | — | cliffs |

(vii) Words ending in 'o' usually form their plurals by adding 'es', e.g.,

| potato | — | potatoes |
| volcano | — | volcanoes |

(viii) Some words do not change in the plural. These include wild animals, birds and fish and some words ending in 's', e.g.,

sheep; deer; trout.

(ix) Some words have no singular, e.g.,

scissors; binoculars.

(x) There are many plurals which come from foreign languages which are irregular, e.g.,

| datum | — | data |

7.   **The problem of compound words and their plurals.**

   (i) When the word relates to men and women both parts go plural, e.g.,

manservant	—	menservants
woman-servant	—	women-servants

   (ii) When there are nouns and adjectives only the noun is in the plural, e.g.,

court-martial	—	courts-martial
tragi-comedy	—	tragi-comedies

   (iii) When there are two titles both become plural, e.g.,

Lord Justice	—	Lords Justices

   (iv) When there are nouns and phrases only the first noun becomes plural, e.g.,

brother-in-law	—	brothers-in-law
Bill of Exchange	—	Bills of Exchange

   (v) Most nouns which are hyphenated change only the second half when plural, e.g.,

ice-cream	—	ice-creams
barrow-boy	—	barrow-boys

WORD-LISTS

The following lists of words include difficult spellings, words with silent letters, foreign words brought into the language and difficult plurals. Whilst the lists are not exhaustive they contain most of the words which cause difficulties for the average student.

Words commonly mis-spelt

Absence
accommodation
achievement
acknowledgement *or*
   acknowledgment

acquaintance
acquiese
acquire
acquit
adder

address
advertisement
aerial
aesthetic
affect
alibi
alligator
allotted
anaemic
analogy
analyse
anniversary
apron
Arctic
argument
aspirin
athlete
audience
auxilliary

Barber
barometer
bedlam
believe
benefitted
bicycle
biennial
blancmange
breakfast
Britain
buoyant
business

Café
calculate
camouflage
campaign
cancel
candidate

canter
carburettor
carnation
cauliflower
ceiling
cemetery
cenotaph
cereal
character
chief
chocolate
choice
choir
choose
chose
cirrus
colloquial
combatant
comet
committed
companion
comparatively
complement
compliment
concise
conductor
connection
conscientious
contemporary
continually
costermonger
council
counsel
coupon
criticism
crucifix
cumulus
cupboard
cylinder

Daisy
decapitate
deceit
deceive
definite
dependant
desolate
diaphragm
dilapidated
diptheria
disappear
disapprove
disciple
discusses
disease
dispelled
draught

Embarrassed
eminence
encore
endeavour
endorse
enquiry
exaggerate
exalted
exhaust
exhibition
extract

Facilities
February
finally
foliage
foolscap
foreign
foretell
forty
fourteen
fulfil

furlong
furtive

Gaffer
gladiator
goodbye
government
grammar
grotesque
guarantee
gypsy

Halibut
handicap
harness
height
heretic
humorous
hydrogen
hygienic

Illegible
immediately
immerse
immigrant
impossible
indictment
ineligible
inquiry
instalment
intimidate
irascible
irresponsible
isosceles
italics
its (of it)
it's (it is)

Jealous
journey

Kaleidoscope
khaki
kindergarten
knot
know
knowledge

Laboratory
laburnum
labyrinth
leisure
library
lieutenant
liqueur
literary
literature
loosely
lose
lunatic
luncheon

Mackerel
maintenance
manageable
manoeuvre
mantlepiece
manufacture
mathematics
meander
medicine
medieval
Mediterranean
megaphone
metalled
microphone
milliner
miniature
miracle
miscellaneous
mischievous

mistletoe
molar
mountebank
muscle

Nausea
navy
necessary
negligible
neice
neigh
nephew
newt
nocturne
noticeable

Occasion
occasionally
occurred
occurrence
octagon
orang-outang

Palate (mouth)
palette (paints)
panic
paraffin
parallel
paralysis
parliament
passed
pasteurize
perambulator
perimeter
permissible
pharmacy
philanthropic
philharmonic
physical
physics

physique
piano
picnic
picnicking
piece
pinnacle
playwright
pneumatic
pomegranate
porcelain
portfolio
possession
practise
predict
preferred
prejudice
presence
principal
principle
privilege
procedure
profession
professor
programme
prominent
pronunciation
propeller
prophecy
prophesy
psalm
pseudonym
psychology
punctual
putrefy
pyramid

Quarrel
queue
quintessence

Raspberry
receive
recognize
referring
representative
rhinoceros
rhododendron
rhythm

Sacrilegious
salary
satellite
scintillate
secondary
seize
separate
Shakespeare
shepherd
similar
souvenir
spaniel
spinster
stationary
stationery
stimulus
suburban
success
successful
supersede
surprised
surprising
symbol

Tandem
tawdry
temporary
terrestrial
terrier
their
there

Unanimous
unconscious
unicorn
unique
unnecessary
until

Vaccinate
vacuum
variegated
veterinary
vinegar
volume

Weather
Wednesday
weird
whether
woollen

Xylophone

Yacht
yield

Zoological

'—able' or '—ible'

'—able'

adorable
advisable
agreeable
amenable
amiable
arguable
bearable
believable
changeable
chargeable
comfortable
conceivable
debatable
definable
desirable
detestable
drinkable
dutiable

eatable
endurable
excitable
forgettable
forgivable
immovable
impenetrable
impressionable
inconceivable
incurable
indispensable
irreconcilable
justifiable
likable
lovable
manageable
movable
namable

notable
noticeable
peaceable
probable
ratable
reasonable
regrettable
removable
serviceable
soluble
teachable
tenable
treasonable
uncontrollable
undeniable
unmistakable

'—ible'

accessible	edible	perceptible
admissible	eligible	permissible
audible	fallible	persuasible
collapsible	feasible	plausible
comprehensible	flexible	repressible
contemptible	gullible	responsible
corruptible	indelible	reversible
credible	inexhaustible	suggestible
deducible	intelligible	suppressible
defensible	irresistible	susceptible
discernible	llegible	tangible
divisible	negligible	visible

'—ence' or '—ent'

'—ence'

absence	difference	providence
confidence	existence	reference
convalescence	preference	residence
correspondence	presence	reverence
defendence		

'—ent'

efficient	insistent

'—ance' or '—ant'

'—ance'

acceptance	attendance	insurance
ambulance	extravagance	maintenance
assistance	grievance	performance
assurance	importance	relevance

'—ant'

accountant	occupant	tolerant
lieutenant	sergeant	

11

Uncountable nouns

These nouns have neither singular or plural. Examples:

accommodation	chaos	electricity
admiration	clothing	employment
advice	comfort	enchantment
aggression	commerce	encouragement
agitation	common sense	endurance
agriculture	compassion	energy
air (atmosphere)	conduct	enthusiasm
amazement	confusion	equipment
ammunition	conscription	espionage
anarchy	constancy	evidence
anger	cordiality	excitement
anguish	counsel	fiction
anxiety	countryside	filth
applause	courage	fish
approval	cowardice	flux
architecture	craftsmanship	fodder
arrogance	cruelty	fog
assistance	cutlery	folly
astonishment	damage	food
attention	debris	foresight
automation	demur	freedom
awe	despair	freight
baggage	dessert	fuel
bait	dirt	fun
behaviour	discomfort	furniture
bewilderment	discouragement	gaiety
bigamy	disillusionment	garbage
blackmail	dismay	generosity
bloodshed	disorder	give-and-take
booty	dissent	gossip
boredom	distress	grammar
bravery	drudgery	gratitude
calligraphy	earthenware	greed
capital (cash)	education	guidance
caviare	effeminacy	gunfire
censorship	elegance	handwriting

harm
harness
headway
health
heat
help
heroism
hesitation
hilarity
honesty
hope (generally)
hospitality
hostility
humanity
humidity
humility
hunger
hysteria
ignorance
illiteracy
immorality
imprisonment
impudence
information
initiative
innocence
insolence
invective
jealousy
jeopardy
jewellery
joviality
junk
jurisprudence
justice
lassitude
laughter
legislation
leisure
lethargy

liberty*
lightning
literacy
litter (rubbish)
loot
luck
luggage
lumber
machinery
magic
magnificence
mail
merchandise
merriment
mirth
mischief
mist
modesty
moisture
money
morality
music
negligence
news
nonsense
normality
notoriety
oblivion
obstinacy
penitence
permanence
permission
perplexity
phlegm
photography
pity*
plunder
poetry
poultry
poverty

practice
pride*
privacy
produce
progress
propaganda
prudence
psychology
publicity
recognition
refreshment
refuse
remorse
research
resentment
rivalry
romanticism
rubbish
rubble
sabotage
safety
sagacity
sarcasm
scaffolding
scenery
sculpture
seaweed
servitude
shame*
shrapnel
slavery
snuff
sobriety
sorcery
stamina
stationery
strength
strife
stupidity
sunlight

sunshine	treatment	weather*
supervision	uncertainty	wisdom*
suspense	upholstery	witchcraft
tact	valour	work
tension	vegetation	worry
thunder	vengeance	worth
traffic	vermin	wrath
transport	wartime	zeal
trash	wealth	

*NOTE the following idioms;

liberty	—	to take liberties;
pity	—	what a pity;
pride	—	take a pride in something;
shame	—	what a shame;
weather	—	to go out in all weathers;
wisdom	—	a wealth of wisdom.

Words with silent letters

almond	knickers	stalk
benign	knocker	succumb
bomb	knife	talk
campaign	knight	thumb
chalk	knit	womb
climb	knoll	wrath
comb	knot	wren
could	know	wrest
design	knuckle	wretched
dumb	lamb	wriggle
feign	malign	wring
folk	numb	wrinkle
foreign	psalm	wrist
half	reign	write
knave	resign	wrong
kneed	salmon	wrote
knell	sign	wry
knew	sovereign	yolk

Plurals

Some '—o' and '—oes' words.

calico — calicoes
cargo — cargoes
domino — dominoes
echo — echoes
mango — mangoes
Negro — Negroes

no — noes
potato — potatoes
tomato — tomatoes
tornado — tornadoes
volcano — volcanoes

But:

albino — albinos
archipelago — archipelagos
bamboo — bamboos
banjo — banjos
cameo — cameos
canto — cantos
concerto — concertos
crescendo — crescendos
cuckoo — cuckoos
curio — curios
dynamo — dynamos
embryo — embryos
fiasco — fiascos

folio — folios
halo — halos
inferno — infernos
kilo — kilos
magneto — magnetos
manifesto — manifestos
memento — mementos
photo — photos
piano — pianos
radio — radios
solo — solos
studio — studios
torso — torsos

Some words that do not change in the plural

barracks
brace
buffalo
deer
gallows
giraffe

grouse
herring
means
mews
pheasant
salmon

series
sheep
species
swine
trout

Some words that have no singular.

aesthetics
anaesthetics
annals
bellows

belongings
binoculars
braces (trouser)
cattle

drugs
economics
goings on
makings

15

mathematics	scissors	thanks
outskirts	shears	tong
pants	shorts	travels
pincers	statistics	trousers
pliers	suds	tweezers
police	surroundings	victuals
politics	takings	winnings

Some irregular plurals

FROM GREEK

analysis — analyses

axis — axes

basis — bases

crisis — crises

criterion — criteria

hypothesis — hypotheses

oasis — oases

phenomenon — phenomena

thesis — theses

FROM LATIN

addendum — addenda

agendum — agenda

appendix — appendices

bacterium — bacteria

datum — data

erratum — errata

genus — genera

index — indices (in mathematics)

index — indexes (lists of contents)

larva — larvae

memorandum — memoranda

nebula — nebulae

person — people

radius — radii

stratum — strata

terminus — termini

FROM HEBREW

cherub — cherubim or cherubs   seraph — seraphim or seraphs

FROM ITALIAN

concerto — concertos

conversazione — conversazioni

dilettante — dilettanti

FROM FRENCH

chateau — chateaux   Mrs — Mesdames
Mr — Messieurs (Messrs)

FROM ARABIC

djinn
genic   — genii

Other plurals

abacus — abaci
alga — algae
alto — altos
alumnus — alumni
antirrhinum — antirrhinums
antithesis — antitheses
apex — apexes (or -ices)
aphis — aphides
appendix — appendices (to
    books, etc)
appendix — appendixes
    (anatomical)
aquarium — aquaria (or -iums)
armadillo — armadillos
autobahn — autobahns
automaton — automata
ay — ayes ('The Ayes have it')
bacillus — bacilli
bamboo — bamboos
banjo — banjos (or -oes)
beau — beaux
bonus — bonuses
buffalo — buffalo (or -oes)
bus — buses
cactus — cacti
calix — calices
cannon — cannon (or -ons)
cargo — cargoes
chipolata — chipolatas
commando — commandos
concerto — concertos

contralto — contraltos
corrigendum — corrigenda
coup d'etat — coups d'etat
crematorium — crematoria
crocus — crocuses
crux — cruces
cupful — cupfuls
dado — dadoes
desideratum — desiderata
desperado — desperadoes
dictum — dicta
dodo — dodos
domino — dominos (cloaks)
domino — dominoes (the game)
dragoman — dragomans
dwarf — dwarfs
dynamo — dynamos
echo — echoes
effluvium — effluvia
elf — elves
embargo — embargoes
emporium — emporia
encomium — encomiums
enigma — enigmas
equinox — equinoxes
Eskimo — Eskimoes
euphonium — euphoniums
facsimile — facsimiles
factotum — factotums
fait accompli — faits accomplis
falsetto — falsettos

fish — fishes *or* fish
flamingo — flamingoes
fly — flies (the insects)
fly — flys (the vehicles)
focus — focuses (foci in
  scientific contexts)
folio — folios
forum — forums
fresco — frescoes
fulcrum — fulcrums
fungus — fungi
gas — gases
genius — geniuses
genus — genera
geranium — geraniums
gladiolus — gladioli
grotto — grottoes
gymnasium — gymnasiums
halo — haloes
handful — handfuls
handkerchief — handkerchiefs
harmonica — harmonicas
harmonium — harmoniums
hero — heroes
hippopotamus — hippopotam-
  uses (or -mi)
hoof — hoofs
hors-d'oeuvre — hors-d'oeuvre
hydrangea — hydrangeas
igloo — igloos
impetus — impetuses
impresario — impresarios
innuendo — innuendoes
isthmus — isthmuses
kilo — kilos
laburnum — laburnums
lacuna — lacunae (or -as)
larva — larvae
lasso — lassos
lay-by — lay-bys

libretto — libretti or librettos
linoleum — linoleums
loofa — loofas (sometimes
  spelt -fah(s))
Lord Justice — Lord Justices
Lord Lieutenant — Lord
Lieutenants
Lord Mayor — Lord Mayors
Lady Mayoress — Lady Mayoresses
maestro — maestros (or -ri)
magneto — magnetos
mango — mangoes
manifesto — manifestoes
Maori — Maoris
matrix — matrices
mausoleum — mausoleums
maximum — maxima
medium — mediums
  (spiritualist(s))
memento — mementoes
memorandum — memoranda
menu — menus
Mikado — Mikados
minimum — minima
minus — minuses
  (for the sign)
momentum — momenta
mongoose — mongooses
mosquito — mosquitoes
mother-in-law — mothers-in-law
motto — mottoes
mulatto — mulattos (-oes)
mummy — mummies
naiad — naiads
narcissus — narcissi (or -uses)
nostrum — nostrums
nucleus — nuclei
nuncio — nuncios
oaf — oafs
oasis — oases

octavo — octavos
octopus — octopuses
omnibus — omnibuses
oratoria — oratorios
pagoda — pagodas
parenthesis — parentheses
parvenu (e) — parvenu(e)s
  (the e for the feminine)
peccadillo — peccadillos
pendulum — pendulums
pergola — pergolas
phenomenon — phenomena
phobia — phobias
photo — photos
piano — pianos
piccolo — piccolos
pick-me-up — pick-me-ups
plateau — plateaux
plus — pluses (the sign)
Poet Laureate — Poets Laureate
polyanthus — polyanthuses
portfolio — portfolios
portico — porticoes
portmanteau — portmanteaus
  (or -x)
potato — potatoes
premium — premiums
prima donna — prima donnas
prospectus — prospectuses
proviso — provisos
purlieu — purlieus
quarto — quartos
quiz — quizzes
quorum — quorums
quota — quotas
rabbi — rabbis
radio — radios
radius — radii
ranunculus — ranunculuses
referendum — referendums

rhino — rhinos
rhinoceros — rhinoceroses
rhododendron — rhododendrons
rhombus — rhombuses
roebuck — roebuck
roof — roofs
rostrum — rostrums
rota — rotas
rotunda — rotundas
saga — sagas
salmon — salmon
salvo — salvoes
sanatorium — sanatoria
sari — saris
scarf — scarfs
schema — schemata
scherzo — scherzos (or -zi)
seraglio — seraglios
serf — serfs
series — series
serum — sera
shako — shakos
shampoo — shampoos
sheaf — sheaves
sheriff — sheriffs
siesta — siestas
silo — silos
simile — similes
sinus — sinuses
ski — skis
solarium — solariums
  (sometimes -ia)
solo — solos
soprano — sopranos
spatula — spatulas
species — species
spectrum — spectra
spermatozoon — spermatozoa
sphinx — sphinxes

spoonful — spoonfuls
staccato — staccatos
stadium — stadiums
staff — staffs
stamen — stamens
stand-by — stand-bys
stanza — stanzas
stiletto — stilettos
stimulus — stimuli
studio — studios
stylo — stylos
stylus — styluses
subpoena — subpoenas
substratum — substrata
surplus — surpluses
syllabus — syllabuses or syllabi
symposium — symposia
synopsis — synopses
tableau — tableaux (sometimes -s)
taboo — taboos
talisman — talismans
tango — tangos
tattoo — tattoos
taxi — taxis
terra-cotta — terra-cottas
  (or -uses)
tiara — tiaras
timpano — timpani
tiro — tiros
tobacco — tobaccos
toga — togas
tomato — tomatoes
tornado — tornadoes
torpedo — torpedoes

torso — torsos
trade union — trade unions
trapezium — trapeziums
trauma — traumata
tremolo — tremolos
trio — trios
triumvir — triumvirs (or -viri)
trousseau — trousseaus
tuba — tubas
tumulus — tumuli
turf — turfs
two — twos
tympanum — tympana
tyro — tyros
ultimatum — ultimatums
Utopia — Utopias
vacuum — vacuums (but vacua
  in scientific contexts)
veranda(h) — veranda(h)s
vertebra — vertebrae
veto — vetoes
virago — viragos
virtuoso — virtuosi
virus — viruses
vista — vistas
volcano — volcanoes
volte-face — volte-faces
vortex — vortices
wharf — wharfs (or wharves)
will-o'-the-wisp — will-o'-
  the-wisps
yogi — yogis
zero — zeros
zoo — zoos

Some foreign words have two plurals — their original and an English plural, e.g.,

bureau	bureaux	bureaus
curriculum	curricula	curriculums
formula	formulae	formulas
sanatorium	sanatoria	sanatoriums

PRACTICE QUESTIONS

1. Add the correct endings to the following list of words.

plenty — ful	boy — ish	carry — age
merry — ly	enjoy — ment	annoy — ance
rely — able	multiply — cation	vary — able
victory — ous	sleep — ness	vary — ous
undeny — able	ignominy — ous	sticky — est

2. To each of the following words add the correct suffix omitting a letter when necessary.

humour (-ous)	labour (-ious)	enter (-ance)
winter (-y)	carpenter (-y)	repeat (-ition)
encumber (-ance)	disaster (-ous)	impetuous (-ity)
tiger (-ess)	curious (-ity)	humour (-ist)

3. Add the correct endings to the following:

advantage — ous	manage — able	behave — iour
embrace — ed	peace — able	love — able
disparage — ment	grace — ious	tire — some
arrange — ing	courage — ous	please — ure
trace — ing	age — ing	save — iour

4. Add the correct endings -*ance* or -*ence* to the following words.

confid —	disobedi —	maintain —
obedi —	perform —	pres —
accept —	abs —	viol —
toler —	insure —	assist —
impertin —	grieve	

5. Supply the missing letter (if any) in the following words.

math — matics	min — ature	fatig — e
develop — ment	a — quaintance	spac — ous
courag — ous	priv — lege	pig — on
embar — ass	dialog — e	ar — tic
scen — ry	vag — e	haras —

6. Choose the correct word from the alternatives given in the following. Explain the meaning of the word you do *not* choose.

(i) Do not trespass or you will be (persecuted, prosecuted).

(ii) 'Romeo and Juliet' is one of Shakespeare's plays (prescribed, proscribed) for the examination.

(iii) Despite his assertion to the contrary, there was no doubt that the soldier was (absent, abstinent) without leave.

(iv) A work of art is often praised for its(ascetic, aesthetic) qualities.

(v) When the gamekeeper appeared with a gun the poacher told us he was not afraid but for all his (bravery, bravado) I know he was quietly terrified.

(vi) The cricketer was well known for his batting and scored a (century, centenary) in the last match.

(vii) Lasa fever is a particularly (contiguous, contagious) disease which is still being researched to find a cure.

(viii) Unfortunately, due to inflation, money values (deprecate, depreciate) annually.

(ix) A judge has to be (disinterested, uninterested) in any case that comes before him because he has to sentence any person where (guilt, gilt) has been established.

(x) Despite the central heating and the electric fire we were still cold as we could not eliminate the (draft, draught) from the room.

(xi) When the soldier died in battle his Colonel praised his bravery in a short (epithet, epigram, epitaph) which read, 'Brave in life and in death'.

(xii) Winston Churchill, an illustrious member of the Marlborough family, was a (famous, infamous) politician of the twentieth century.

7.   Rewrite the following extract, correcting all mis-spellings:

We were forced to weight for Gerald and Tom who were not dew to arrive untill seven. With time hanging hevy on our ands we decided to aproach a small restarant which we new was neerby. Brian drove his car skilfully and altho there was little or no parkin space he managed to get it neetly alongside the kerb and proceded to lock it up securly. We jumped out quikly and immediatly went into the cafe and ordered butered scons. We had no arguements about wot to eat becos we both licked scons. Once we had finished our snak we recieved and payed our bill of fair and went back to the plaice were we where positiv we would meat our freinds.

8.   Correct the spelling of the following words (if necessary).

accomodate; woolen; pavillion; emmigrate; laborotory; effervese; embarass; fulfil; forfiet; dipthong; haras; goverment; parlement; calender; Britian; benefitted; anonemous; buisnes; garantee; mischievious; necesary; whiring; yaght; vacinate; umberella; picknic; comparitive; litterature; Shakspear; medecine.

DIRECT AND INDIRECT SPEECH

There are two ways in which a speech or conversation can be reported. The exact words can be repeated or the words can be introduced by a verb in the past simple tense, e.g.,

The writer said that . . . **or** He said that . . .

If the first method is used we say that it is written in **direct speech.** If the second method is used it is said to be **reported** or **indirect speech.**

GENERAL RULES

Direct Speech		**Reported Speech**
Present Simple	*becomes*	Past Simple
Present Continuous	*becomes*	Past Continuous
Present Perfect Simple	*becomes*	Past Perfect Simple
Past Simple	*becomes*	Past Perfect Simple
Present Perfect Continuous	*becomes*	Past Perfect Continuous
Past Continuous	*becomes*	Past Perfect Continuous
Future	*becomes*	Past Perfect Continuous

THUS:

Direct Speech		**Indirect Speech**
He is	*becomes*	he was
He can	*becomes*	he could
He may	*becomes*	he might
He is making	*becomes*	he was making
He makes	*becomes*	he made
He was throwing	*becomes*	he had been throwing
He has found	*becomes*	he had found
He will go	*becomes*	he would go
He will have gone	*becomes*	he would have gone
He would go	*becomes*	he would have gone
He was missed	*becomes*	he had been missed

MUST

'Must' may be used in four different ways in direct speech and therefore has four forms in reported speech.

(i)   **Habit** (must - had to)

I **must** always change into my boiler suit to go to work.
Bill said that he always **had** to change into his boiler suit to go to work.

(ii)   **Future action** (must - would have to)

You **must** take notice of what your parents say.
His brother told him he **would have to** take notice of what his parents said.

(iii)   **Permanent arrangement** (does not change)

You must take the handbrake off first.
She said that he must take the handbrake off first.

(iv)   **A prohibitive command** (must not - was not to or must not)

You **must not** go out without an umbrella.
Her mother said that she **was not to** go out without an umbrella.
or
Her mother said that she **must not** go out without an umbrella.

Ought to, should and **used to** do not change.

PARTICULAR WORDS AND PHRASES

Direct Speech		**Reported Speech**
Today	*becomes*	that day; the same day
Yesterday	*becomes*	the day before; the previous day
Tomorrow	*becomes*	the day after, the following day
The day before yesterday	*becomes*	two days before
The day after tomorrow	*becomes*	in two days' time
This; these	*becomes*	that; those; (the)
now	*becomes*	then; at that time; immediately; at once.

Direct Speech		Reported Speech
Here or hither or hence	*becomes*	there, thither or thence
Last night	*becomes*	the previous night
Ago	*becomes*	before
Here	*becomes*	there; in that place
Last week	*becomes*	the week before; the previous week
Next week	*becomes*	the week after; the following week

Commands

The imperative in a direct command is changed to an infinitive in an indirect command, e.g.,

> "Hurry up, Harry!"
>> His uncle told Harry to hurry up.
> "Don't shoot!"
>> The captive forbade the soldier to shoot.

Exclamations

There are no rules to help in changing exclamations into reported speech. Their form depends on their meaning only, e.g.,

> "What a superb circus!"
>> He remarked on the excellent quality of the circus.
> "How foolish you are!"
>> He commented on my foolishness.

Particular expressions

Certain words and expressions cannot be expressed exactly in reported speech, e.g. please, Oh! Now then! Really! Indeed! Help! They have to be put into reported speech in this way, e.g.,

> "Help! the house is on fire!"
>> She screamed for help as the house was on fire.
> "Put the kettle on, please."
>> He asked her politely to boil the kettle.

Similarly, it is sometimes necessary to supply an opening phrase, e.g.,

"I am sorry that I could not come. I had another patient whom I had to see.

The doctor apologised for his absence. He explained that he had to see another patient.

REPORTED TO DIRECT SPEECH

Generally, the remarks listed above apply in reverse. Remember, the past perfect simple tense can be changed to present perfect or past simple. Remember also to use inverted commas, commas and appropriate paragraphing. Where necessary introduce colloquial abbreviations into the direct speech, e.g.,

The bus driver told the passengers they would be leaving in half an hour.
"We'll be leaving in half an hour," said the bus driver.

EXAMPLES

1.   Re-write the following discussion in reported (indirect) speech.

John   Did you enjoy the concert last night?

Mary   Yes, very much. But I thought that the last singer went on a bit too long. I missed my train and I had to stay the night with a friend.

John   Perhaps so. I was pleasantly surprised to find the School Hall so full. These concerts are not usually so popular.

Mary   Most people prefer bingo these days. I am looking forward to the poetry reading next week. Some of the poems are on the syllabus of my English literature examination and I hope I shall understand them better afterwards.

John   I am not taking English literature but I shall certainly go to the reading.

ANSWER

John asked Mary if she had enjoyed the concert the night before.

27

Mary replied that she had but thought that the last singer had taken too long to finish and so she had missed her train and had had to stay with a friend for the night. John agreed but said that he was pleasantly surprised to find the School Hall so full because these concerts were not usually so popular. Mary pointed out that most people prefer bingo but that she was looking forward to the poetry reading the following week: some of the poems were on the syllabus of her English literature examination and she hoped that she would understand them better afterwards. John said that he was not taking English literature but that he would certainly be going to the reading.

2. The following is adapted from Kenneth Grahame's *Wind in the Willows*. Re-write it showing what each character says (that is, change this passage in indirect speech into direct speech):

Badger continued that the Wild Wood was pretty well populated with all the usual lot and he fancied that Mole knew something about them himself by that time. Mole, with a slight shiver said that indeed he did. Patting him on the shoulder, Badger said that it had been Mole's first experience of them but that he would pass the word around and that any friend of *his* walked where he liked. Rat was anxious to be off and stuck his pistols in his belt again. He explained that they must start while it was daylight but Otter said that he knew every path blindfold and Badger added that there was no need for Ratty to fret.

ANSWER

"The Wild Wood is pretty well populated with all the usual lot," continued Badger. "I fancy that you know something about them yourself by this time, Mole."

"Indeed I do," said Mole with a slight shiver.

Patting him on the shoulder, Badger said, "It was your first experience of them but I will pass the word around and any friend of *mine* walks where he likes."

Rat was anxious to be off and stuck his pistols in his belt. "We must start while it is daylight," he said.

But Otter said, "I know every path blindfold."

"There is no need for you to fret, Ratty," added Badger.

PRACTICE QUESTIONS

1. Rewrite the following telephone conversation in indirect speech:

Please ask your uncle Bob if it will be in order for me to come and see him next Thursday. I understand that he wants to sell his house and as I am moving into the area I might be interested in making an offer for it. Ask him to phone Burslem 58321 to let me know if Thursday is alright. My name is Jack Thomas.

2. Rewrite the following in reported speech:

"Is Miss Allen in the garden, yet, Mary?" inquired Mr. Winkle, much agitated.

"I don't know sir," replied the pretty housemaid. "The best thing to be done, sir, will be for Mr. Weller to give you a hoist up into the tree, and perhaps Mr. Pickwick will have the goodness to see that nobody comes up the lane, while I watch at the other end of the garden. Goodness gracious what's that light?"

"Dear me!" said Mr. Pickwick, turning hastily, "I didn't mean to do that."

"Shut it up, sir, can't you?" said Sam.

"It's the most extraordinary lantern I ever met with, in all my life!" exclaimed Mr. Pickwick, "I never saw such a powerful reflector."

3. Change the following into direct speech:

His speech had become thick and indistinct. Jasper, quiet and self-possessed looked to Neville as if expecting his answer or comment. When Neville spoke, his speech was also thick and indistinct. Defiantly, he said that it might have been better for Mr. Drood to have known some hardships. Edwin, turning merely his eyes in that direction asked why it might have been better for Mr. Drood to have known some hardships. Jasper assented and with an air of interest asked for a reason. Neville replied that the reason was that they might have made him more sensible of good fortune that was not by any means necessarily the result of his own merits. Mr. Jasper quickly looked to his nephew for his rejoinder. Edwin Drood sitting upright then asked if he had known any hardships. Mr. Jasper quickly looked to the other for his retort. Neville replied he had.

FIGURES OF SPEECH AND LITERARY APPRECIATION

Figures of speech or figurative language is the opposite of literal language. Such figures of speech are designed to alter the literal meaning of words, to make a meaning appear fresh and more interesting, to create a sensory effect or to widen the reference of a word or expression. Figurative language makes demands on the imagination of the reader. Thus, if we say that someone is nipping a plan in the bud or that some one has taken the bull by the horns, it is obvious that we are not really speaking about a plant or a bull or a bull's horns. The writer has simply called on our imagination to make comparisons and transfer our ideas (as in similes, metaphors, personification and metonymy) or to realise that he is exaggerating (hyperbole) or that he means the opposite of what he is saying (irony and sarcasm). Besides figures of speech there are other devices of style which depend on how sounds and words are arranged — they might ideally be called figures of arrangement — these are assonance, alliteration, antithesis and onomatopoeia.

METAPHOR

In this figure of speech something is said to be something else, e.g., The moon is a ghostly galleon. We all know the moon is not a ship (galleon) but this is exactly what has been said. In this metaphor both elements of the comparison are given — moon and galleon. Another type of metaphor and most common is where both sides of the comparison are not given, e.g., "The embers of love burned in Rosie's heart."

Here, the metaphor is embers but we have to think before we come to the conclusion that the comparison is between

the embers of love — dying love

and the embers of a fire which are going out, i.e. a 'dying' fire. The comparison is **implied** in the use of the word embers. Below are a few examples of metaphors:

(i) Football is a magnet for thousands every Saturday.

(ii) "My father, he was a mountaineer.
His fist was a knotty hammer"

(Binet)

(iii) "The pale silken ribbons of the rain
Knotted, are fluttering down the window pane"

(Edith Sitwell)

(iv) "All the world's a stage"

(Shakespeare – 'As You Like It')

(v) The mountain crowned the summit of the hill.

(vi) Night was descending and sharp stars pricked the blue.

SIMILE

This is a figure of speech in which two things or actions are compared. The comparison is between things that are different. A simile is usually introduced by the word as or like but this is not essential. All that is needed is that both sides are distinctly stated, e.g.,

The squire was as cunning as a fox.

Here, the comparison is between the man (the squire) and the animal's cunning (the fox)

A few more examples of similes are:

(i) "Sudden a thought came like a full-blown rose,
Flushing his brow, and in his pained heart
Made purple riot . . ."

(Keats – 'The Eve of St. Agnes')

(ii) "And like a lobster boiled, the morn
From black to red began to burn"

(Samuel Butler)

(iii) "A rare bird on the earth and very like a black swan."

(Juvenal)

(iv) "Like infant slumbers, pure and light"

(John Keble)

(v) Curses are like young chickens,
they always come home to roost

(Robert Southey)

31

PERSONIFICATION

This is a figure of speech in which inanimate or abstract things are given the qualities of a person or treated as if they were humans, e.g.,

Can Honour's voice provoke the silent dust?

Here Honour is said to have a voice as if this attribute could speak. Similarly in Longfellow's "Daybreak" he says of the wind,

"It whispered to the fields of corn,
Bow down, and hail the coming morn"

Further examples are as follows:

(i) "Close bosom friend of the maturing sun"

(Keats)

(ii) "Who hath not seen thee oft amid thy store?
Sometimes whoever seeks abroad may find
Thee sitting careless on a granary floor
Thy hair soft-lifted by the winnowing wind."

(Keats)

(iii) "Night's candles are burnt out, and jocund day
Stands tiptoe on the misty mountain tops"

(William Shakespeare)

(iv) "Poetic Justice, with her lifted scale,
Where, in nice balance, truth with gold she weighs
And solid pudding against empty praise."

(Alexander Pope)

(v) "The Old Lady of Threadneedle Street in danger."

(James Gillroy)

OTHER COMMON FIGURES OF SPEECH

METONYMY

This is a figure of speech in which the name of something associated with an object is substituted for it, e.g.,

the kettle is boiling (i.e. the water in the kettle)

Hyperbole

This is a figure of speech in which exaggeration is used for emphasis, e.g.,

> "Will all great Neptune's ocean wash the blood
> Clean from my hand? No; this my hand will rather
> The multitudinous seas incardine,
> Making the green one red."

> *(Shakespeare – "Macbeth")*

Litotes

This is a figure of speech in which understatement is used for emphasis, e.g.,

> He is a citizen of no mean city. *(i.e., He is a citizen of a very large city.)*

Paradox

This figure highlights an apparent contradiction, e.g.,

> If you drive on the left in this country you are right. *(i.e., The correct side of the road to drive in this country is on the left.)*

Oxymoron

This is the bringing together of apparently contradictory words, e.g.,

> The music stopped and we were met with an eloquent silence.

Euphemism

This is a figure which expresses unpleasant things in a less unpleasant form, e.g.,

> He has passed away. *(i.e. He had died.)*

Antithesis

This figure of speech brings together two sharply contrasted ideas, e.g.,

> Fools rush in where angels fear to tread.

Synecdoche

This figure uses a part to signify the whole, e.g.,

> The farmer lost twenty head of cattle in the hurricane.

Irony

This suggests the opposite of what the words imply when taken literally, e.g.,

> You are a clever boy aren't you. *(A teacher to a dull pupil when he is anything but clever.)*

Apostrophe

This is a figure of speech in which a person or personified idea is addressed directly, e.g.,

> "Milton! thou shouldst be living at this hour"

> *(William Wordsworth)*

FIGURES OF ARRANGEMENT

Assonance

This is a device which repeats the rhyming of vowels but not of consonants e.g., feet; bean; seen and been. Certain catch phrases and proverbs use the device e.g., a stitch in time saves nine. In verse it produces a musical effect.

Alliteration

This is a device which repeats the same letter or sound in successive words or syllables, e.g.,

> "The long light shakes across the languid lake."

Where statements are balanced one against the other implying contrast this is called balanced antithesis.

Onomatopoeia

This is a poetic device in which the sense is suggested by the sounds of the words used, e.g., "The bare, black cliff clanged round him" — the knight's armour is striking the rock.

Climax

This is the arrangment of a series of statements in increasing order of importance, e.g.,

> The horse started to trot, then broke into a canter until it was finally galloping headlong across the beach.

Anticlimax

This is the opposite of climax involving a sudden descent to something quite trifling, e.g.,

> The bomb destroyed the House of Lords, a row of departmental stores, a plush theatre and my new hat.

SOME SIMILES IN CURRENT USE

There are many similes in current use. A list of some is given below and you should read and re-read it to familiarise yourself with them.

as agile as a monkey
as bitter as gall
as black as coal (or soot)
as blind as a bat
as bold as brass
as bright as a lark (or button)
as brittle as glass
as brown as a berry
as busy as an ant (or bee)
as calm as a cat
as changeable as the weather
as clean as a new pin
as clear as a bell (or crystal)
as cold as ice (or charity)
as cool as a cucumber
as crafty as a fox
as cunning as a fox
as dead as a doornail (or mutton)
as deaf as a post
as devoted as a mother

as dry as a bone
as dull as ditchwater
as easy as winking (or A.B.C.)
as fast as a hare (or deer)
as fat as butter (or a pig)
as feeble as a child
as fierce as a lion
as fit as a fiddle
as flat as a pancake (or a flounder)
as fleet as a gazelle
as fresh as a daisy (or paint)
as frisky as a two-year-old
as gentle as a dove (or a lamb)
as good as gold
as graceful as a swan
as green as grass
as hairy as a gorilla
as happy as a king (lark or sandboy)
as hard as iron (horn or nails)
as harmless as a dove
as heavy as lead (or an elephant)
as hot as a furnace (or fire)
as hungry as a hunter (or wolf)
as keen as mustard
as large as life
as light as a feather
as like as two peas (or herring)
as loyal as an apostle
as mad as a hatter (or a March hare)
as meek as a lamb
as obstinate as a mule
as old as the hills (or Methuselah)
as open as day
as pale as death
as patient as Job
as plain as a pikestaff
as playful as a kitten (or puppy)
as pleased as Punch
as plump as a partridge
as poor as a church mouse

as proud as a peacock
as purple as the heather
as quick as lightning
as quiet as a church mouse
as red as a beetroot (or turkey-cock)
as regular as a clock
as right as rain
as round as a barrel (or an orange)
as safe as houses (or the bank)
as sharp as a needle (or razor)
as sick as a dog
as silent as the grave
as silly as a sheep
as slippery as an eel
as slow as a snail (or a tortoise)
as smooth as glass (or velvet)
as sober as a judge
as soft as butter (or down)
as sound as a bell
as sour as vinegar
as steady as a rock
as stiff as a poker
as stolid as a cow
as straight as an arrow (or a ramrod)
as strong as a horse (or an ox)
as sturdy as an oak
as sure-footed as a goat
as sweet as honey (or sugar)
as swift as a deer (hare, or hawk)
as tall as a giant
as tenacious as a bulldog
as tender as a chicken (or a shepherd)
as thick as thieves
as thin as a rake (or lath)
as timid as a mouse (or rabbit)
as tough as leather (or old boots)
as true as gospel (or stick)
as ugly as sin
as warm as wool
as weak as water
as white as snow
as wise as an owl (or Solomon)
as white as a sheet (snow or a ghost)

Other similes are introduced by like. A few are:

like chaff before the wind
climb like a monkey
fall like a blanket
flounder like a fish out of water
like a bull in a china shop
look like a bundle of old rags
ran like a bull at a gate
run like the wind (or deer)
run like wildfire
sold like hot cakes
stampede like a herd of elephants
swim like a fish
the sea was like glass
tremble like a leaf
walk like a panther stalking a deer

Similes are invented constantly and while many of those listed have become stereotyped it is possible to invent your own carefully thought out images. A few such similes from famous writers are:

"Feebly she laughed in the languid moon,
While Porphyro upon her face doth look,
Like puzzled urchin on an aged crone."

"A vile conceit in pompous words express'd
Is like a clown in regal purple dress'd."

"This city now doth *like a garment wear
The beauty of the morning.*"

"Day after day, day after day
We stack, nor breath nor notion
*As idle as a painted ship
Upon a painted ocean.*"

SOME FIGURATIVE EXPRESSIONS

Many figures of speech have been repeated so often that we hardly notice them. Many figurative expressions have become so over-used that they are now clichés. While it is wise to know what they mean they should not be used too much in your written work and unless you can find a fresh, stimulating image it is best to stick to literal language. (Additional expressions will be given in the vocabulary sections.)

Figurative Expression	Meaning
to live from hand to mouth	to exist under difficult conditions
to lend an ear	to listen
to turn a deaf ear to	to ignore
to clear the air	to explain
to make an ass of yourself	to act foolishly
to make a pig of yourself	to be greedy
to give yourself away	to betray your thoughts
to get your back up	to become annoyed
to jump at the bait	to be quick to be attracted to something which aims to deceive
to have a bee in your bonnet	to have an unreasonable conviction or desire
to have bats in your belfry	to be abnormal (or mad)
to tighten your belt	to make economies
to kill two birds with one stone	to accomplish two things with one action
a fly in the ointment	an obstacle or hindrance
to have a bone to pick	to have something to quarrel about
to take the bull by the horns	to face up to a threat or danger
to have the trump card	to have the initiative to take action which will bring reward

Figurative Expression	Meaning
to show one's true colours	to show one's real nature
cupboard love	love or affection to gain something
a dead letter	something, often a rule or law, no longer observed
to get cold feet	to be afraid
to play second fiddle	to have an inferior role
to be light fingered	to steal
to come round	recover consciousness
to fall out	to quarrel
to hold up	to rob
to run the gauntlet	to have to face excessive danger
to go against the grain	to be against one's feelings
to get the upper hand	to gain control
to skate on thin ice	to do something which will get you into trouble
to be on your mettle	to be well prepared
to be out of sorts	to feel ill
to look for a needle in a haystack	to look for something almost impossible to find
a hard nut to crack	a person or problem difficult to deal with
to put one's shoulder to the wheel	to make an effort
to be on the rocks	to be destitute or in difficulty
to give somebody the cold shoulder	to snub or ignore someone
to be at sixes and sevens	to be confused
to call a spade a spade	to speak bluntly
to pull up the ladder	to cut off help from a person

Figurative Expression	Meaning
to be under somebody's thumb	to be under a person's control
to toe the line	to do as you are told
to hold your tongue	to be quiet
to pull the wool over somebody's eyes	to deceive
to clutch at a straw	to seize at any slender chance of getting out of difficulties
an eye-opener	a revelation
a blackleg	a person who continues to work during a strike
lady-killer	a man who believes he is irresistible to women
night-cap	an alcoholic drink at bed-time
an open secret	not a secret at all
a slowcoach	someone who works or moves slowly
a deadlock	an impasse
a makeshift	an inferior substitute
a red rag to a bull	something which arouses and antagonises another
a mouthpiece	somebody who says what he is told
eyewash	a fale story intended to deceive
to escape scot-free	to get away completely and without injury
a wild-cat scheme	a speculative, far-fetched venture
to put the clock back	to take a retrograde step
to keep a stiff upper lip	to suffer difficulties without complaint
to read between the lines	to deduce from assumed facts

Figurative Expression	Meaning
to be out of the wood	to escape from difficulties
a square peg in a round hole	somebody in a job or position which does not suit him.

EXAMPLE

Below is a worked exercise on appreciation of poetry. First, read the poetry two or three times to make sure you understand it and then answer the questions in sequence referring to the poetry each time.

WHEN FLOWERED MY JOYFUL SPRING

Whilome in youth, when flowered my joyful spring,
Like swallow swift I wandered here and there;
For heat of heedless lust me so did sting
That I of doubted danger had no fear:
I went the wasteful woods and forests wide,
Withouten dread of wolves to been espied.

I wont to range amid the mazy thicket,
And gather nuts to make me Christmas game,
And joyed oft to chase the trembling pricket,
Or hunt the heartless hare till she were tame
What reckèd I of wintry age's waste?
Tho' deemèd I my spring would ever last.

How often have I sealed the craggy oak,
All to dislodge the raven of her vest?
How have I wearied with many a stroke
The stately walnut-tree, the while the rest
Under the tree fell all for nuts at strife?
For ylike to me were liberty and life

Edmund Spenser

(a) What stage in his life is the poet recalling?

(b) What dangers existed in the forest according to the first verse? Why was the poet not aware of them?

(c) What figure of speech is used in the first verse, second line? Explain the comparison. Why is it so apt?

(d) What device is used in the second verse, line 5?

(e) Explain the significance of the line,
"Tho'deemèd I my spring would ever last."

(f) What response, if any, is the poet expecting to get to the questions in the last verse?

(g) Explain the words (i) whilome (line 1); (ii) lust (line 3); (iii) wasteful (line 5); (iv) pricket (2nd verse line 3); (v) heartless (2nd verse line 4) and (vi) ylike (last verse, line 6).

ANSWERS

(a) He is reminiscing about his youth when he played in the woods.

(b) They were lonely and isolated and wolves roamed about. The poet was not aware of these because he was enjoying himself so much.

(c) The figure of speech is a simile. The poet is comparing himself to a bird. It is apt because a bird flies from tree to tree and the poet explains the fun he had in trees when a youth.

(d) This is the device known as rhetorical question, a question which does not require an answer.

(e) The young boy was so happy that he thought his fun and games in the forest would last forever.

(f) None, the questions are rhetorical. He is pointing out the numerous times he tried to collect birds eggs and walnuts.

(g) Whilome — formerly; lust — pleasure; wasteful — lonely; pricket — buck; heartless — timid; and ylike — alike.

PRACTICE QUESTIONS

1. Consider the poem below and then answer the questions which follow it.

AT THE SETTING OF THE SUN

Come all you young fellows that carry a gun,
Beware of late shooting when daylight is done,
For 'tis little you reckon what hazards you run,
I shot my true love at the setting of the sun.

In a shower of rain as my darling did lie
All under the bushes to keep herself dry,
With her head in her apron I thought her a swan,
And I shot my true love at the setting of the sun.

I'll fly from my country, I nowhere find rest
I've shot my true love like a bird in her nest.
Like lead on my heart lies the deed I have done,
I shot my true love at the setting of the sun.

In the night the fair maid as a white swan appears
She says, O my true love, quick dry up your tears,
I freely forgive you, I have Paradise won,
I was shot by my love at the setting of the sun.

O the years as they pass leave me lonely and sad,
I can ne'er love another and naught makes me glad.
I wait and expect till life's little span done
I need my true love at the rising of the sun.

  (i) The poem tells a sad story — explain it. Why isn't it entirely sad?

 (ii) The last verse is particularly pathetic. Why?

(iii) What lesson is the poet trying to put across to others?

(iv) What figures of speech are used in the 3rd stanza. Explain them.

(v) Despite the fact that she has died the true love re-appears. Explain.

(vi) What iş the poet looking forward to himself in the last stanza? Explain the use of the word rising instead of setting in the last line of the poem.

2. What figures of speech or devices of style are used in the following? Explain any comparisons.

(a) "Slowly, silently, now the moon
Walks the night in her silver shoon"

(Walter de la Mare)

(b) "Sweet Auburn! loveliest village of the plain"
(Oliver Goldsmith)

(c) "A good book is the precious life-blood of a master spirit, embalmed and treasured up on purpose to a life beyond life."
(John Milton)

(d) "Madam, a circulating library in a town is an evergreen tree of diabolical knowledge."

(Richard Brinsley Sheridan)

(e) "Milton! thou shouldst be living at this hour
England hath need of thee; she is a fen
Of stagnant waters"

(William Wordsworth)

(f) "Tyger! Tyger! burning bright
In the forests of the night.
What immortal hand or eye
Could frame thy fearful symmetry."

(William Blake)

(g) "O, my Luve's like a red red rose
That's newly sprung in June
O my Luve's like the melodie
That's sweetly play'd in tune."

(Robert Burns)

(h) "Sceptre and crown
Must tumble down,
And in the dust be equal made
With the poor crooked scythe and spade.

(Percy Bysshe Shelley)

(i) "And I will love thee still, my dear,
Till a'the seas gang dry:
Till a'the seas gang dry, my dear,
And the rocks melt wi' the sun."

(Robert Burns)

(j) "Busy old fool, unruly sun,
Why dost thou thus . . ."

(John Donne)

(k) "O Wild West Wind, thou breath of Autumn."
(Percy Bysshe Shelley)

(l) "Who hath not seen thee oft amid thy store?
Sometimes whoever seeks abroad may find
Thee sitting careless on a granary floor,
Thy hair soft-lifted by the winnowing wind."

(John Keats)

3.   What 'figures of arrangement' are used in the following?

(m) "The fair breeze blew, the white foam flew,
The furrow followed free."
(Samuel Taylor Coleridge)

(n) "Reading maketh a full man; conference a ready man; and
writing an exact man."

(Francis Bacon)

(o) "The moan of doves in immemorable elms
and murmuring of innumerable bees."
(Alfred, Lord Tennyson)

4.   Define the following giving an example of each:

metaphor, simile, metonomy, hyperbole, alliteration, assonance, onomatopoeia.

5.   Write sentences using each of the following words metaphorically.

(i) black; (ii) cold; (iii) root; (iv) key; (v) door.

6.   Explain the following figurative expressions:

(i) To live from hand to mouth;

(ii) to turn turtle;

(iii) to rush from pillar to post;

(iv) to set sail;

(v) by hook or by crook;

(vi) to turn in;

(vii) to stick to one's guns;

(viii) to be run down;

(ix) to pull wool over someone's eyes;

(x) to pull one's socks up;

(xi) to pass out;

(xii) to make hay while the sun shines;

(xiii) to make a mountain out of a molehill;

(xiv) to make a clean breast of something;

(xv) to keep something up one's sleeve.

. 7.   Complete the following similes as they are usually written:

(i) As sound as . . .

(ii) as bold as . . .

(iii) as dull as . . .

(iv) as safe as . . .

(v) as fit as . . .

(vi) as dead as . . .

(vii) as . . . as ink

(viii) as . . . as a cucumber

(ix) as . . . as a hatter

(x) as . . . as saffron

(xi) as . . . as punch

(xii) as . . . as lightning

8.   What do we infer about a person when we call him:

(i) A shark

(ii) a monkey

(iii) a worm

(iv) a snake

(v) a mouse?

ESSAY WORK

In this section we shall consider certain aspects of written work in some detail. These are **Letter Writing, Writing Stories, Writing Descriptions** and **Report Writing.**

LETTER WRITING

Letters are one of the most important means of communication and millions of letters go through the mail daily. Letter writing can be divided into two main types — personal or business.

Personal letters

These are informal communications and are written either in answer to some enquiry, request, invitation or to acknowledge a gift; or in order to send personal news and opinions to relations or friends.

General rules

(i) A personal letter while informal should be grammatically correct. The tone may be intimate.

(ii) If your friend asks any queries remember to answer them.

(iii) Make your letter interesting by writing about friends and places you both know.

(iv) If you are writing a 'thank you' letter say how pleased you are with the gift. Pick out particular features that make the gift especially useful and acceptable. If you are expressing thanks for hospitality include reminiscences of particular incidents or places that you enjoyed.

(v) Do not apologise for your writing, the kind of ink or pen used or the poor quality of the writing paper. It is insulting to suggest that you have not given your friend the best you can.

(vi) Do not over-use the personal pronoun 'I'. Do not begin by saying "I am writing to you" for this is obvious.

(vii) It is not necessary to include the name and address of the recipient at the beginning of the letter.

(viii) It is a good idea to work out a plan of campaign for personal letters. Thus, if you are writing in response to a query or request the plan could be:

Introduction	Refer to the request.	(1 paragraph)
Body	Write a detailed answer to the request.	(2-3 paragraphs)
Conclusion	Personal message or greetings.	(1 paragraph)

If you are writing a personal letter to a friend or relative the plan could be:

Introduction	Preliminary greetings and response to previous correspondence.	(1 paragraph)
Body	Current news, opinions and reasons for them. Future intentions.	(3-6 paragraphs)
Conclusion	Personal enquiries and messages.	(1 paragraph)

(ix) Typical beginnings and endings of personal letters are:

Friends	*Salutation (beginning)*	*Subscription (ending)*
Casual	Dear Joe,	Yours sincerely,
Close friends	My dear Joe,	Yours very sincerely,
Intimate	My dearest Joe,	Your best friend,
Relations		
Distant	Dear Cousin Bob,	Yours affectionately,
Close	My dear Uncle Bill,	Your affectionate nephew/niece,

Other subscriptions that can be used are:

Your friend,	Your loving daughter,	Your loving son,
Yours ever,	Your affectionate	With best wishes
Best wishes,	friend,	from,

(x) Note in the salutations the capital *D* and *J* in Dear Joe: also note the small *d* in My dear Joe.

(xi) Note the capital *Y* and small *s* in Yours sincerely. (There is no apostrophe in **Yours.**) There is no comma except after sincerely. Be careful about the spelling of sincerely.

(xii) The Christian (first) name is sufficient if the recipient knows you well. If you address a person by name in the salutation e.g., Mr. Jones, you end with Yours sincerely.

Planning a personal letter

The letter should begin on the line below the salutation. A general plan for personal letters is as follows.

1st paragraph	Reason for Writing.
2nd-5th paragraphs (This varies according to subject matter.)	Details
Last paragraph	Personal messages, greetings and inquiries.

When writing this kind of letter in an examination you are expected to write clear English. The letter must therefore be grammatically correct as well as the punctuation. It is wise to avoid slang and if you have to use a word like "stunning" put it in inverted commas.

An example of a personal letter

Hotel Splendide,
Jersey,
Channel Islands.
3rd June, 1981.

My dear Uncle Bob,

I have now been in Jersey three weeks and felt I had to write to tell you how I was getting on here. As you paid for my six weeks vacation I thought it was only right to tell you how I have enjoyed myself and to thank you once again for all you have done for me.

The journey here was uneventful for I boarded the 'Sealink' with my small car at Weymouth. Fortunately — for you know I am a very poor sailor — we had a very smooth crossing. I spent my time partly on the deck, reading newspapers and magazines and eating in the ship's restaurant. The food was, I must admit, very good indeed and I enjoyed every bit of it, I ate so much that I did not get hungry for the whole of the journey which was about eight hours. When the ship left the U.K., it was drizzling and I was pleasantly surprised when we arrived in St. Helier because the sun was shining.

Since I have been here, the weather has remained sunny and bright. Only a few days have been warm though and only on those days have I been able to use the hotel pool. Besides swimming I have walked a great deal and have visited nearly every important part of the island with my rucksac on my back. I have abandoned my car by day but have used it to go out to the cinema and shows at night.

Yesterday, I visited the German museum here which I found most interesting. I was reminded that you were a despatch rider during the last war and I wondered what it was like. In the bunker there were German vehicles, rations, equipment and weapons which all seemed rather 'old-fashioned' to me: I suppose it is because I was born into the nuclear-weapon age. Near the German bunker is a motor museum — a miniature Beaulieu. I was surprised to see how many British cars they had. Like you Uncle Bob, I am interested in engines and I stayed there almost two hours.

At the end of the first week I met a girl my own age and we were attracted to each other as soon as we could get up enough courage to speak. Her name is Elizabeth and she comes from Worcester. I was surprised to hear her Birmingham accent and teased her about it but actually I have become used to it now and must say I like the way she speaks. Last night we went to a Disco and we danced all the evening. We had a very good time indeed and left for the hotel at 3 in the morning. It is a good job I did not have to get up for work this morning!

The food here has been first-class and nothing is too much trouble for the staff. I have had poultry for dinner each day and the fish foods have been splendid. Just the food for the 'Hotel Splendide' I suppose! Writing about food has reminded me that it is lunch time and I had better go downstairs so that I do not miss the meal. Afterwards I expect to go for a stroll before having a game of squash with Elizabeth.

Before I finish please remember me to Aunt Millicent and give her my fondest wishes. Should you see Dad tell him I am having a good rest and that I am thinking about him and especially Mum. I hope that she has recovered from her bronchitis now and that she received the flowers that I sent her.

Your affectionate nephew,

James.

Informal invitation

"Nusquama",
4, Utopia Road,
Eldorado.
2nd February, 1982.

Dear Mary,
I am holding a small party next Wednesday, the 5th February, at my home. It is my birthday and I hope that you can come. The party should start about 7 p.m. and will probably go on until midnight. I shall probably wear jeans. Please let me know if you can join us.

Yours sincerely,

Jane.

Letter in reply to an Invitation

21, Cowslip Lane,
Flotsam,
Lilliput.
3rd February, 1982.

Dear Jane,

Thank you for your invitation to your birthday party on Wednesday, the 5th February at your home. I shall be delighted to come. I shall catch the 6.30 'bus and should arrive about 6.50 p.m. I am looking forward to seeing you and all our friends.

Yours sincerely,

Mary.

Letter of thanks

"Nusquama",
4, Utopia Road,
Eldorado.
29th December, 1982.

Dear Uncle George,

Thank you for the fountain pen. It is a most acceptable Christmas present and you may be sure that I shall make good use of it. Father says that with such a pen I am bound to pass my examinations.

Please give my love to Aunt Gladys. I hope we shall see both of you soon.

Your affectionate nephew,

John.

BUSINESS LETTERS

Formal correspondence includes:

> Letters to a firm, making enquiries or complaints.
>
> Letters from a firm, giving information or dealing with complaints.
>
> Circular letters.
>
> Letters of application for employment.
>
> Letters to some one who is unknown to you making a request or enquiry.
>
> Letters to a magazine or newspaper.
>
> Invitations and acceptances in connection with some event or function.

The style of a business letter is formal and follows a set of rules which must be learnt.

(i) The letter should be brief but must contain all relevant information and give precise dates and exact quantities.

(ii) Write your address in full at the *top right hand side* of the page. Do not write your name there. Each line of the address should be indented. Put a comma after every line except the last, then put a full stop. A comma after a house number is optional.

(iii) On the next line below the address write the date in full — e.g., 1st June, 1981. That is day, month, year with a comma after the month and a full stop after the year. The day should be directly underneath the first letter of the first line of the address. Remember that 1st, 2nd, 3rd, 4th etc., are **not** abbreviations and so no full stop is required after them. There are several ways of writing the date:

12th January 19 —	12th Jan. 19 —
Jan 12th, 19 —	January 12th, 19 —
12. 1. 19 —	

(iv) On the next line (the line below that used for the date) write the name and address of the person or the firm the letter is going to: this should be on the left-hand side of the page. The first letter of each line comes directly under the first letter of the line above and against the margin.

(v) When writing to an individual the title Esq. is often used, e.g., John Jones, Esq. Do not write Mr. and Esq. together — this is a serious error.

(vi) Remember that the address of the recipient inside should agree exactly with the name and address on the envelope. The title 'Messrs' should be used only when the company includes a personal name.

(vii) "Dear Sirs" should be used when a letter is addressed to a firm. If addressed to one person, use "Dear Sir" or "Dear Madam". See later.

(viii) Give a reference if there is one, and the date of the most recent relevant correspondence. Be impersonal and brief. NOTE: if writing for goods do not ask the firm to send them to "the above address", they will do this, anyway. If writing for a position with a firm, do not ask for an interview. If thought suitable you will get one. Do not "beg to apply for the post of". This is too humble.

(ix) Generally speaking business letters end with "Yours faithfully". Note the capital Y and the small f. "Yours truly" may also be used (but see later for other beginnings and endings).

(x) 'Mr.' need not be added to the signature but 'Mrs.', 'Ms' or 'Miss.' should be placed in brackets after the name when the writer is female.

Consider the following:

Messrs. T. Jones & Co., Ltd.,
The Rainbow Printing Company, Ltd.,
The Secretary, **or** The Manager,
    Messrs. Thomas, Evans, Ltd.,
R.A.Wilson, Esq., **or** Mr. R.A.Wilson.,
Sir R. Cresswell, O.B.E., M.A.,
The Rev. R. Williams.,

The Rt. Hon. A. Walpole, M.P.,
Dr. R. Thomas, **or** R. Thomas, Esq., M.D.,

Note that titles and decorations are placed before university degrees.

(xi) Beginning and Ending Business Letters.

Type of Formal Letter	Salutation	Subscription
Sent to an individual	Dear Sir, (Madam,)	
Sent to a firm	Dear Sirs, (Mesdames,)	Yours faithfully,
Sent to a committee or board	Dear Sirs, or Gentlemen,	
Circular	Dear Sir, (Madam,)	
To a firm of solicitors	Gentlemen,	
To directors of a firm	Gentlemen,	
To a distant acquaintance	Dear Mr. Y,	Yours truly, or
To a person on the same level as you	(Dear Mrs. Y,)	Yours sincerely,
To an editor of a magazine/newspaper	Dear Sir, or Sir, (Dear Madam, Madam,)	Yours truly,

If the letter is addressed to the directors or a firm of solicitors, Gentlemen is the correct salutation. Sir is now regarded as very formal and is used for letters to and from government officials.

(xii) The signature is placed on the line after the subscription. A full signature is required but there is no need to include full christian names unless you normally sign in this way. A person's full signature is usual in formal letters, e.g.,

John F. Randall.

(xiii) When letters are signed by, for example, a manager or secretary on behalf of a firm the abbreviation 'per pro' or 'p.p.' is written. These words mean per procurationem or by delegation to and should be placed before the signature of the person who is signing the letter on the firm's behalf.

(xiv) If you write more than one page, number them.

(xv) Remember to avoid clichés or business jargon.

Business jargon should be replaced by **plain English.**

inst., or instant	of this month
ult., or ultimo	of last month
prox., or proximo	of next month
We are in receipt of your esteemed communication.	
We have to acknowledge receipt . . .	We have received . . .
We beg to acknowledge receipt . . .	
We are in agreement . . .	We agree . . .
Re. (Latin for "concerning the matter")	With reference to . . .
Furnish all necessary particulars.	Give details.
Kindly advise us as to your wishes.	Please let us know what you want (or require).
Enclosed herewith please find . . .	We are enclosing . . .
We hereby beg to inform you . . .	We wish to inform you . . .
Attached hereto . . .	Attached . . .
In connection with . . .	About
. . . only too pleased to . . .	. . . glad to . . .
We have now received *the same* . . .	We have now received *it*
. . . at your earliest convenience.	. . . as soon as possible.

Planning business letters

Like a personal letter, the business letter proper should begin on the line below the salutation and should be indented. All subsequent paragraphs should be indented so that they are all an equal distance from the margin. A few plans are suggested for you.

Plan of a letter of complaint

1st paragraph	The reason for writing.
2nd-3rd paragraphs (May vary according to nature of complaint)	Details of complaint.
Last paragraph	Request for action.

Plan of a letter of enquiry

1st paragraph	The reason for writing.
2nd-3rd paragraphs (varies)	Details of enquiry.
Last paragraph	Request for help.

Plan of a reply from a firm giving information

1st paragraph	Reasons for writing.
2nd-3rd paragraphs (varies)	Nature of information.
Last paragraph	Suggestions.

Plan of a letter dealing with a complaint

1st paragraph	Reason for writing, e.g., in response to a complaint.
2nd-3rd paragraphs (varies)	Details of action suggested either by: (a) complainant *or* (b) firm complained about.
Last paragraph	Actual action taken.

Plan of a letter of application

1st paragraph	Reason for writing. Refer to vacancy and how you came to know about it.
2nd-3rd paragraphs (varies)	Details of previous relevant experience including education and previous employment. If no experience suggest why you should be considered.
Last paragraph	Details of present position and copies of testimonials or reference to where further enquiries about applicant can be made.

Plan of a letter to a newspaper

1st paragraph	Reason for writing — indicate subject to be dealt with.
2nd-3rd paragraphs (varies)	Details of your own views on subject concerned.
Last paragraph	Suggest an action or solution to the problem/s if possible.

Plan of a circular letter

1st paragraph	Reason for writing.
2nd-3rd paragraphs (Varies)	Details.
Last paragraph	Action required by recipients.

Examples of business letters

Letter to a firm

23, Acacia Avenue,
Hounslow,
Middlesex.
20th August, 1980.

The Service Manager,
Hotspur Electrics Ltd.,
12-13, Longfellow Street,
Hounslow.

Dear Sir,

Last year I bought one of your Hotspur De Luxe spin drying machines and it has worked well until now. I am sorry to say that I have recently had considerable trouble with it.

In the first place, some screws have come loose from the body of the machine and two have actually dropped off so that the machine is almost falling to pieces. Secondly, the spin drier is not working properly and when I take the clothes out they are still very wet. Thirdly, when I use the machine it makes a peculiar whining noise and the whole house seems to shake as it reverberates. Your engineer who came to give it a service recently said when he left that it was in perfect working order.

In view of these circumstances I should be glad if you would send me one of your other service engineers as soon as possible to repair the machine. I am, of course, willing to pay any reasonable expenses to get the machine in working order again.

Yours faithfully,

(Mrs.) Elizabeth Sellars.

Letter from a firm

Speedy-Link Ltd.,
12, High Street,
Holywell,
Peebles.
10th September, 1981.

O.K. Valves Ltd.,
1350, Thirty-Second Street,
Pittsburgh,
Pennsylvania,
U.S.A.

Dear Sir,

Reference the valve parts for the machines which we manufacture and further to our letter ordering 5,000 'V' shaped valves, 5mm.

In view of the fact that we have had a further substantial order for our complete machines I should be grateful if you would send us as soon as possible a further 10,000 of the same valves. Thus, the amended order should read,

15,000 'V' shaped valves with a diameter of 5mm.

Please let us know as soon as possible when these can be shipped, if possible by Telex. Thank you for your help in this matter, I am,

Yours faithfully,

D. Robert Peabody, Secretary.

A letter of application

14, Everest Road,
Newtown,
Glasgow.
3rd November, 1980.

The Manager,
'Buy Your Own Home' Building Society Ltd.,
14, High Street,
Glasgow.

Dear Sir,
      Reference your advertisement in the "Glasgow Herald" of 2nd November, 1980 for a clerk to help in your general office from 1st December, 1980. I wish to apply for the position.

I am 18 years of age and was educated at the Glasgow Comprehensive School from 1973 — 1978, and sat for the General Certificate (Lowers) Examination in my last term at school. I passed in English, mathematics, physics, chemistry, history and French (with oral proficiency). Since leaving school I have been working full-time for a shipping company and during the evenings have been studying part-time for business qualifications. I can, therefore, type and take shorthand but I have also been studying commerce and management.

My present salary is £50 per week with free luncheon vouchers. I am keen to find a position which offers me opportunity for advancement. I enclose copies of testimonials from:

A.C. Davies, Esq., M.A., Headmaster, Glasgow
Comprehensive School.

D.C. Wiseacre, Esq., B. Com., Head of Commerce
and Business Studies Department, Glasgow College
of Further Education.

The Rev. C. Blandford, St. Mary's Vicarage, Glasgow.

My present employers have kindly agreed to answer any inquiries you may wish to make.

Yours faithfully,

(Miss) A. Davies.

NOTE the difference between a testimonial and a reference. A *testimonial* is a report on a person's character, ability or suitability given to the employee who usually keeps the original and sends copies with his letters of application. A *reference* is a report on a person's character and ability sent to prospective employers but is *NOT* given to the employee.

Letters in response to an application

Acceptance

'Buy Your Own Home'
Building Society Ltd.,
14, High Street,
Glasgow.
18th November, 1980.

Miss Anne Davies,
14, Everest Road,
Newtown,
Glasgow.

Dear Miss Davies,

Reference your application for the position of clerk with us to help in our general office and your attendance for interview here on the 14th November, 1980.

I was very pleased with your attitude and the way you dealt with the short written test I gave you. I have much pleasure in confirming your employment with us. Please come to the office at 9 a.m. on 1st December, 1980 and I will introduce you to your colleagues.

The salary for the position is £60 per week. Working hours are 9 a.m. until 5 p.m. with alternate Saturdays off and holidays are three weeks annually. The appointment will be subject to seven days notice either side but there will be a probationary period of three months. With best wishes,

Yours faithfully,

A. Hope, Manager.

Letter to a newspaper

"The Mount",
4, Endicott Place,
Summerville,
Worcester.
4th January, 1981

The Editor,
"Daily Satisfaction",
Fleet Street,
London, EC4.

Dear Sir,
      I have never before been sufficiently roused to write a letter to any newspaper but John Doe's report headed "Legal ineptitude" has provoked me to do so.

It is not that Mr. Doe's account was so grossly inaccurate but the fact that he only wrote about one aspect of a solicitor's work that upset me most.

Until a few years ago I had had no dealings at all with solicitors, my knowledge was gleaned only from the Press, and my father led me to believe that they were dilatory, that they lived in expensive mansions, charged excessive fees and were not wholly to be trusted. This may be true of some members of the legal profession but I am sure it is a small minority.

Solicitors work long and hard. The average day lasts from 9 a.m. until 7 p.m. Then there is the excessive paper work. The solicitors in the practice where I work spend nearly every Saturday morning at the office trying to catch up.

It is not a well-paid profession, despite the responsibility involved. It seems to me to be an endless battle between this and that matter and this and that court-case or brief.

Thus, I felt I had to put in a good word for solicitors as more than most professions they are maligned and abused. Unfortunately, most of them do not have the time to defend themselves.

Yours faithfully,

A.B.Roose.

A circular letter

Star Grocers Ltd.,
Sebastopol Street,
St. Helens,
Lancashire.
20th September, 1981.

Dear Sir or Madam,

With the high-cost of foodstuffs and the difficulty of getting transport into the centre of the town — and even if you have your own transport the difficulty of parking once you get there — you might well be wondering how you are going to get your household supplies this winter.

We stock all the leading brands of foodstuffs. To name only a few Heinz and John West canned goods, McDougalls flour, Tate and Lyle sugar, Typhoo Tea, Nescafe and Maxwell House coffee and a wide variety of all sorts of foods, household utensils and things for every home. We serve our customers in a well heated, convenient supermarket and we employ staff to help you choose exactly what you want. In essence, we operate a supermarket with the added bonus of a personal service. Our costs are very competitive and we have over one hundred different items on offer each week.

May we, therefore, invite you to visit our new supermarket? We are sure you will not be disappointed and assure you our aim is to be of service always.

Yours faithfully,

p.p. Star Grocers Ltd.,
H.H. Tasty.
(Managing Director)

Letter to an individual making a formal request

4, The Cut,
Ridgeway,
Cirencester.
4th November, 1981.

Dear Brigadier Williams,

As honorary secretary of the Ridgeway Photographic Club, I am arranging a series of short talks for my members beginning in January, 1982. We all know that you are an enthusiastic amateur photographer and that some of your photographs have been so good that they have appeared in national magazines. Mr. Roger Stone, who you know, has suggested that I approach you.

The membership of the Ridgeway Photographic Club has grown from a mere six members when it was formed in 1976 to over forty-five members and we have our own purpose built rooms for meetings, taking shots and dark-room techniques adjoining the Youth Club. If you agree to come I am sure there will be a good turnout.

The short talks will start with members of the club participating in January and I have kept February open until I hear from you. We normally meet on Fridays and if you could make it on any Friday evening in that month at 7.30 p.m. I would be most grateful.

If you find it possible to accept this invitation during the month suggested I shall be glad if you will let me know. If you can come, perhaps you would let me know what equipment you will need if any. We have our own slide projector, film projector and dark-room equipment but if there is anything additional you will need I shall be very pleased to provide it.

Yours truly,

E.M. Rowe,
(Honorary Secretary)

A formal invitation

This should be written in the third person as follows:

The Governors and Principal of Beckley College of Further Education request the pleasure of the company of Mr. and Mrs. D. Bowen at the Prize-giving ceremony, to be held in the College Hall on February 21st 19——, at 8.00 p.m.

R.S.V.P.

A formal acceptance

Mr. and Mrs. D. Bowen thank the Governors and Principal of Beckley College of Further Education for their kind invitation to the College Prize-giving and have much pleasure in accepting it.

A formal refusal

Mr. and Mrs. D. Bowen thank the Governors and Principal of Beckley College of Further Education for their kind invitation to the College Prize-giving but due to a previous engagement they are unable to attend.

ADDRESSING ENVELOPES

(i) Begin the address about a third of the way down and towards the left hand side of the envelope. The first letter of each line should be a little to the right of the first letter in the line above. Enough space should be left for the stamp and for post office franking.

(ii) In general, there is a comma at the end of each line, with a full stop at the end of the last line and after all abbreviations.

(iii) Do not use "Mr." and "Esq." together. Remember that a comma comes before "Esq.".

(iv) Decorations are written before degrees. If there are two decorations, remember that civil honours come before military, e.g.,

F.C. Jones, Esq., O.B.E., (civil honour) D.F.C., (military honour) M.A. (degree).

The addressed envelope should appear thus:

> The Manager,
> Frazer and Co., Ltd.,
> Booksellers,
> 21, Fitzroy Street,
> EDINBURGH.

(v) The postcode must be the last thing you write in the address, and should preferably be on a line by itself. The postcode is written in capitals and no dots or punctuation of any kind should be added to it.

(vi) The following are examples of the ways in which envelopes may be addressed, with the relevant postcodes.

> Mr. W. Smith,
> 514, Kingsbridge Road,
> DERBY.
> DE1 8ZL

> G. Penter, Esq.,
> 49, Memorial Road,
> ORPINGTON,
> Kent.
> BR6 9UA

G. Jones, Esq., O.B.E., B.A.,

Managing Director,

Toys for Children Ltd.,

Unit 4,

Cwmbran Trading Estate,

SWANSEA.

West Glam.

SA4 36

WRITING STORIES

Writing a story is difficult to do well. In essay work for examinations you only have time and space to tell a *short* story so learn to do this quickly and efficiently. Lengthy descriptions, detailed, full-length character studies and long-winded painting of scenery is out. Arouse your reader's interest immediately. Once he reads the first few lines he must be made eager to continue.

Remember that dialogue can add vividness to narrative work. Make it crisp, pointed and natural. To write dialogue successfully you have to have a clear mental picture of your characters. Conversations in everyday life have interruptions, sudden changes of theme and people have their own particular quirks and idiosyncracies. Listen carefully to people talking and include words and phrases you hear in your work. A talkative person will make long often 'boring' speeches, more frequently than a quiet character. The latter tends to speak in short sentences or monosyllables. Short conversations can be used to convey character — a bully will interrupt and shout; an uncouth person will yawn in your face; a pompous person will use long words slowly and like the sound of his own voice; a timid person will hardly speak; a fast-thinker is likely to talk quickly, etc. But the variables are enormous.

Unlike other types of written work, in dialogue you are allowed to use abbreviations — won't, can't, shan't, I'm, it's — and colloquialisms and slang are acceptable (in moderation). Such language helps to convey colour to your characters. Dialect too, can be used if you can handle it. Thus, if you live in Wales, the West Country, the North

Country or Scotland you might be able to give your characters some local flavour as well. In this connection, read some of the work of Dylan Thomas, Thomas Hardy or Robert Burns. As for the spelling of such dialects, the principle is to spell words or phrases phonetically — that is the spelling should be as near to the actual sounds of the words as you can get it.

The simplest kind of story is the anecdote — the very short story. This is often funny or witty but it can be macabre or very serious. It is a good idea to write short pieces like this when you start writing narratives and then to build on these in future work. An example of an anecdote appears below.

A Tall Story

During the last war an enemy agent landed in a remote village in South Wales called Penclawdd. His first task was to contact the local spy, Dai Jones, and their method of identification was to quote the code-words, 'The fish are biting in Penclawdd Bay'. When the enemy agent enquired where Dai lived he discovered there were five Dai Joneses in the village. He decided to contact each one in turn. He knocked at the home of the first Dai Jones and a small boy came to the door. He was told that Dai Jones was not at home because he was working on the afternoon shift. To save calling again the agent asked the small boy to give Dai a message – 'The fish are biting in Penclawdd Bay'.

The small boy replied immediately "You have the wrong house. You want Dai Jones the spy. He lives in number twelve."

When writing a story vary the length of your sentences and remember that very short sentences used one after the other serve to speed up a narrative while very long sentences serve to slow it down. Try not to use 'and', 'then' and 'so' too frequently. Generally speaking you should use the past tense.

The ending is important. Read the short stories of famous writers — Guy de Maupassant, Chekhov, O. Henry and Somerset Maugham to name only a few — and see how they complete their efforts. The technique of the 'punch line' is a good way to end or alternatively you could use a surprise ending.

Finally, if you write a story in the form of a play, dialogue becomes paramount. In such a story too, it is necessary to give stage directions. These are always given in the *present* tense and it is usual to describe the scene and characters *before* the conversation opens. Sometimes it is necessary to indicate the period of time in which the scene is set and also the time of day, or of night.

Rid your mind of television series or films you have seen when writing narratives. Many of these, for example, "The Incredible Hulk", "Crossroads" and "Coronation Street" use 'formula' techniques and copying these will make your work commonplace. Description, narrative and dialogue are essentials but your story must have a point to it — this is often called the *climax* by writers and can appear in the middle or at the end. Some clever writers start with the climax and then tell the story — but this is unusual and the element of surprise is lost.

WRITING DESCRIPTIONS

Writing descriptions is not easy. Book 1 has an example of describing a scene which is the simplest of all the descriptive techniques. Here, we must say something about describing simple objects, processes and actions, events, people and animals, as well as describing scenes and places.

Describing simple objects

Where possible try to have the object in front of you. If you can touch it and if it is not too heavy or precious or fragile pick it up. Examine it closely when it is in your hands. Consider if it is like any other object you know.

If you do not have the object before you close your eyes and visualise it mentally. Then, follow a plan. A typical plan is:

1. Name the object and define it in the opening line/s.

2. State the purpose of the object.

3. Consider the structure of the object. Describe its properties if relevant — structure, shape, size, weight, colour, general appearance.

4. If the object has separate parts with different functions describe and explain them.

5. If possible make comparisons with other similar objects.

Most important in all describing methods is the ability to make quick and accurate definitions. This involves the summing up of the essentials and expressing them in as few words as possible. The following will help you:

(i) A definition consists of one sentence only.

(ii) It is a good thing to say what class of things the object belongs to first.

(iii) The characteristic distinguishing the object defined from other classes is important and completes the definition.

Examples of correct definitions

(i) Eye: the organ of sight.

(ii) Nose: the organ of smell.

(iii) Solicitor: a person qualified to give advice on legal matters.

(iv) Physician: a person qualified to give advice on matters connected with the body and its diseases.

(v) Bookcase: a piece of furniture with shelves for holding books.

(vi) Lift: a device by which people or objects are raised or lowered vertically from one level to another.

(vii) Water: a liquid which boils at 100 deg C and freezes at 0 deg C.

(viii) Handkerchief: a material used for wiping and cleaning mucus from the nose.

(ix) Carving knife: a piece of kitchen equipment used for cutting food, especially meat.

(x) Spanner: a tool used for tightening and untightening nuts.

Here are some useful common classifications that will help in your definitions:

a person; a worker; a craftsman; a clergyman; a liquid; a gas; a chemical compound; a fuel; a drink; a food; a cereal; a mineral; a garment; a piece of furniture; a musical instrument; a form of lighting; a form of heating; a cooking device; a profession; an occupation; a tool; an instrument; a device; a container; a piece of kitchen equipment; a metal; a mineral; a substance; a material; a game; a toy; a building; a structure; a construction; a vehicle; a means of communication; a geographical feature; a geometrical figure; a process; a system; a quality; a quantity; a form of literature; a document; a means; a place; an official.

Describing processes and actions

The most important thing to remember when describing processes and actions is to make sure you present facts logically and in sequence. You can write impersonally (e.g., To keep a bicycle tyre in good order, see that the correct pressure is maintained in each tyre.) or you can use a more personal approach. In the last-named you can use the personal 'I' e.g., If I had to paint a room, I should first . . . Alternatively, the reader can be addressed as you.

Again, it is necessary to have a plan of campaign and the following plan might be useful:

1. Preparations — apparatus, equipment or tools.

2. Doing the task — main work.

3. Additional points to remember.

Describing events

These are really descriptions of personal experiences. Thus if you go to a camp or on a long journey or go to a special place on holiday, you might be asked to describe the event. The best way to deal with such an essay is to consider it in chronological order. A typical essay plan follows.

Write a description of your first ride in an aeroplane.

PLAN

Introduction *(1st paragraph)*	Date of flight. Your age when taken. Particulars of place you left and destination.
Body of Essay	1. Take off. Outward journey. Scenery. Places of interest. Food. Your opinion of flying — sensation. The people with you. 2. Arriving at your destination. Brief details of time spent in place you visited. 3. Plane back. Differences between outward journey and this one. Reactions at going home. Arrival at airport.
Conclusion	Final impressions. Would you travel by air again? Do you prefer it to other forms of travelling?

Describing people and animals, scenes and places

In the last three sections we have dealt largely with the description of inanimate objects and occurrences. There are two main methods of describing people, animals, scenes and places. These are called the **objective method** and the **subjective method.**

When you write objectively it means that you write impersonally about something. You write in a purely factual way. To do this you write in the third person. Thus,

> *The Gower is a peninsula in South Wales, approximately ten miles west from the centre of Swansea. It consists of a promontory of fine beaches stretching around the coast the furthest and most beautiful being the long expanse of sand which is known as Rhossili Bay.*

Alternatively, the 'subjective' style may be employed. In this you give your personal views or impressions on the things being described. In this style you would use the first person singular. Thus,

I like the Gower coast it is a beautiful peninsula in South Wales, reached by car (or hiking) ten miles from the centre of that old, neglected, Welsh industrial seaport of Swansea. Incidentally, Swansea is my home town and when I was a child I did not realise that only a stone's throw from it was some of the most beautiful stretches of sand and clear water in the world. The beach I like best is Rhossili where people can swim, paddle or fish from the rocks or practice hang-gliding from the mountains that overlook it.

Journalists often use a third method of presentation of descriptive facts by imaginining that the reader himself is visiting a particular scene, or is describing a person or an animal or a particular place. To do this they use the second person — *You would hardly expect to see . . . It will delight you to realise . . .* Only when you can handle your descriptions and the language well should you attempt this method.

For these types of essays it is only possible to give general plans and the student writer must himself decide in what style he should write — objectively or subjectively.

Plan — describing a person

Introduction	Name of person. Age. Sex. Whether living or dead.
Body of Essay	Physical appearance. Dress.
	Character. Subjective — why you like or dislike the person.
Conclusion	Habits and idiosyncracies.

It is important to select interesting details in your description — details that make your subject different from others.

Plan — describing an animal

Introduction	Type of animal. To what genus it belongs.
Body of Essay	Physical appearance — size. Colour, shape. Particular characteristics. Habits. Peculiarities.
Conclusion	Where found.

Plan — describing a scene or place

Introduction	General remarks about place, position, size and age.
Body of Essay	Details of history. Details of development. Colour, shape. Particular characteristics. Exterior — interior if a building. In sunshine — in rain if outside.
Conclusion	Any points of special interest. What makes it memorable or otherwise.

REPORT WRITING

A report is written work intended to present data so that those asking for the information can act upon it. A report has to be (a) clear; (b) logical and (c) precise. It has to be based on all the information on the particular theme that can be gathered. This includes facts, figures, documents, evidence and opinions. Such data must be sorted and arranged chronologically, then set down and one or a series of recommendations made. Thus, a typical plan for a report would be as follows:

Plan of a Report (which should be in the form of a letter to the person requiring it).

Introduction	The terms of reference — the instructions given. Formal statement that this letter embodies the report.

Body of Essay   The facts from the evidence. Detailed information and all relevant data. This must be logical and chronological.

Conclusion   Recommendations. The writer must himself suggest logical solutions to the problems brought out in the report.

PRACTICE QUESTIONS

Letter writing — personal letters

1. Write a letter to your best friend inviting him to your birthday party.

2. Write a reply to a letter you have received in connection with a short holiday, saying that you cannot come.

3. Your aunt is 95 years old today. Write her a letter congratulating her on her birthday.

4. A close relative of your friend has just died. Write a letter of condolence.

5. Your sister-in-law has just given birth to a baby-boy. Write a letter of congratulation to her and her husband.

6. Your friend has just failed an important examination. Write a letter expressing sympathy.

7. Write a letter to your pen-friend abroad whom you have never met, asking him to come and visit you.

8. A letter has come from your pen-friend asking you to visit. Write a suitable acceptance letter.

9. Your pen-friend is to arrive next week and his plane lands at Heathrow Airport. Give him instructions how to reach you.

10. Write a letter to an ageing relation (uncle or aunt) thanking him for a present received.

Business letters — inquiries/complaints

1. Write a letter to the Automobile Association complaining about a particular route that they recommended to a destination in this country.

2. Write a letter to a travel agency enquiring about the cost of the cheapest holiday they have in Spain.

3. Near your home is a large works which gives off black smoke which has ruined your washing for some weeks. Write (i) a letter to the Local Authority complaining about the nuisance; (ii) a letter to the firm lodging a complaint.

4. The firm mentioned in question 3 has not replied nor has the Local Authority taken any action. Write to your M.P. about the matter, c/o. The House of Commons, Westminster, London.

5. Your neighbour has parties every night keeping you and your family awake until the early hours of the morning. Write a letter of complaint to him.

6. Despite your letter in question 5 to your neighbour, he continues to keep you awake. Write to a solicitor instructing him to act on your behalf. The solicitor is Mr. J. Dent, L.L.B. Solicitor, Borough Chambers, York.

7. A company called the Ace Electric Co., of 4, Stony Stratford Street, Runcorn, has sold you a defective garden hose worth £30. You have refused to pay them and solicitors have written to you pressing for payment. Draft an appropriate reply to the solicitors, Messrs. Bloggs and Bloggs, Solicitors, 10, Pentonville Street, Parkhurst.

8. Your local electricity board has overcharged you for electricity. Your bill should be £10 but they have charged you £110. Write to the following: Secretary to the Board, Middleditch Electricity Board, Runcorn.

Applications

1. You are applying for a new job as a draughtsman. Write an appropriate letter of application to Metal Equipment Ltd., 4, Greenacre Estate, Huddersfield, Yorkshire.

2. You are the personnel officer of a large sweet manufacturing company. You have had fifty applicants for a particular job. After interview you select Alfred Burns. Write a letter offering the job to him at his home address which is 5, Bathurst Street, Halifax, Yorkshire.

3. You are the personnel officer of a large sweet manufacturing company. You have had fifty applicants for a particular job. Forty-nine candidates are unsuccessful. Write a standard letter of rejection to the unsuccessful candidates.

4. Write a letter of application in response to the following advertisement in the *Western Mail.*

    We require an experienced outside salesperson to sell our range of commercial refrigeration, ice-makers, microwave ovens, etc. Excellent position for person who can produce results. Write: Company Secretary, Cane Refrigeration, 4, High Street, Caerphilly.

5. Apply for the following position advertised in the *Daily Telegraph.*

    Managing Director requires efficient secretary. Good shorthand and typing essential. Salary negotiable. Electric typewriter. Staff canteen. Four weeks' holiday. Please apply in writing to Managing Director's Secretary, *Daily Argus,* Pall-Mall, London. SW1.

6. Reply to the following advertisement in the *Daily Telegraph.*

    Flour salesperson required for specialised independent flour mill in East Anglia. Applications plus *c.v. and salary required to the Managing Director, F.S. 8400, *Daily Telegraph,* EC4.

    *c.v. curriculum vitae – up-to-date details of qualifications and experience.

Formal requests/inquiries/acceptances

1.   Your name has been suggested as Chairman of the local debating society. Because of pressure of work you are unable to accept. Write a letter of rejection to your friend who is secretary of the organisation, Mr. John Barnes, Middleway Dramatic Society, Middleton.

2.   You want to order the following from a local stationers —

      4 Parker pens; 2 packets Basildon Bond Stationery; 12 H.B. pencils; 4 reams A5 paper; 4 medium exercise books (ruled). Draft a suitable letter to Hometown Stationery Supplies, 4, The Mount, Beaumaris.

3.   You have just been appointed secretary to the Local Amateur Theatric Society — this is a part time job that you have wanted for some time. Write a formal letter of acceptance to The Hometown Dramatic Society, 4, Shaw Street, Ibsenville.

4.   Write a letter to the organiser of a holiday camp for young people asking if you can come for a fortnight in August.

5.   Draft a letter to the Librarian of your local public library asking him to get you a particular book you need for your studies.

Circulars

Write a circular letter beginning Dear Sir (or Madam) drawing attention to:

1.   a special sale of antiques;

2.   a bring and buy sale;

3.   a Charity Bazaar;

4.   a local Garden Party;

5.   the advantages of joining a club or society of which you are a member.

Letters to the press

1 Write a letter to the editor of your local newspaper:

(i) complaining about the number of salesmen knocking at your door trying to sell you and your family things;

(ii) complaining about the amount of litter on the streets of your town or village;

(iii) complaining about the numbers of dogs roaming around and barking at night.

2. Write a letter to a national newspaper complaining about the present state of education.

3. Draft a letter to a national newspaper praising any local scheme of improvement you know about.

4. Someone has written to a a national newspaper complaining about the state of the economy. Draft a reply saying why you agree or disagree with the letter.

Formal invitations and acceptances

1. You have just been invited to a wedding. Draft a formal acceptance to the parents of the bride, Mr. and Mrs. Fairweather, 4, Blissful Crescent, Merryweather.

2. You have been invited to give a talk to a local Society. Draft a reply accepting the invitation.

3. You are the head of a business firm. Write a formal letter to your Staff inviting them to a Christmas party.

Envelopes

Address envelopes to the following:

1. Mr. J. Jones, 75, Friary Lane, South Street, Derby.

2. The Acme Cleaning Co., Ltd., 75, Priory Street, Nowhere.

3. To John Raikes who is an M.A., Ph.D., and O.B.E., and who lives at 'The Priory', Blandford Close, Suntown.

Dialogues

Write an imaginary conversation between:

1. A sparrow and a cat trying to catch it.
2. A stall-holder in a market trying to overcharge and a customer
3. A bus passenger trying to get on a full bus and the conductor.
4. A policeman stopping a motorist for a minor offence and the motorist.
5. A newspaper vendor and someone buying a newspaper.
6. A race-horse and a cow, comparing their lives.
7. A sailor and an airman, comparing their lives.
8. A farmer and a town-dweller, comparing their attitudes to scenery and the open air.
9. A tortoise and a parrot, comparing their relative positions as pets.
10. A dog and a cat, comparing their modes of life.

Anecdotes

The following lines are extracts from anecdotes that are incomplete. Write a short story to suit each extract including the exact words used at some point in the story. The stories may be serious, humorous or be a combination of these.

1. He searched frantically in all his pockets. In a foreign land and he could not find his passport.
2. His shopping finished, his trolley piled high with goods, the bill made out and he could not find his money.
3. Jack had given her a beautiful ring and now the most important part — the stone — was gone.
4. The cars came towards each other. Nothing could now prevent the crash.
5. We were all on board the ship and a force 10 gale was forecast and imminent.

6. Someone was downstairs. I picked up my heaviest available weapon and crept down slowly to meet him — or it.

7. I rang the bell. I knocked at the door. Nobody answered. I pushed the door gently, and to my surprise, it slowly opened.

8. The girl looked up at him as they danced. 'I am sure I know you', she said.

9. I knew that he was the criminal. And there he was on television before my very eyes, giving an interview.

10. He was extremely angry. As I entered he slammed the door and locked it firmly.

Short stories

Write a short story on one of the following themes:

1. My most embarassing incident.

2. A practical joke that misfired.

3. A curious event.

4. The antics of a child I know.

5. How an old lady (or gentleman)reacted.

6. It pays to be honest.

Write the following well-known stories taken from history in your own words.

7. Sir Robert Bruce and the spider.

8. Julius Caesar arriving in Britain.

9. King Canute trying to stop the tide.

10. Drake playing bowls before the Armada battle.

11. Guy Fawkes and the Gunpowder Plot.

12. Humphrey Davy and his invention of the miner's lamp.

13. Florence Nightingale and her work at Scutari.

14. Fleming and the discovery of penicillin.

Miscellaneous

1. Write the story of any great invention in the past one hundred years.

2. Write a short scene for acting about either (a) life at school or (b) life at work.

3. Examine either (a) a postage stamp or (b) a bank note and write a story about what it tells you.

4. Write a short story on one of the following themes: (a) Hobson's choice; (b) Beginner's luck; (c) Devil's play; (d) Teacher's pet; (e) Prize bully; (f) Mistaken identity.

Descriptions — simple objects

1. Write definitions of the following:

(i) Oxygen;	(vi) a roof;
(ii) a visa;	(vii) a garden spade;
(iii) a policeman;	(viii) porridge;
(iv) a waiter;	(ix) hydrogen;
(v) flour;	(x) an electric torch.

Describe

(i) A table knife;	(vi) a teapot;
(ii) a table fork;	(vii) a walking stick;
(iii) a pair of scissors;	(viii) an umbrella;
(iv) a television set;	(ix) a wrist watch;
(v) a radio;	(x) an alarm clock.

3. Describe in not more than 150 words the following objects and explain simply how each works:

(i) A bicycle;	(vi) a table lighter;
(ii) a sewing machine;	(vii) a water tap;
(iii) a camera;	(viii) a mouse-trap;
(iv) a vacuum cleaner;	(ix) a table lamp;
(v) a thermometer;	(x) a record player.

Descriptions — processes and actions

Describe in not more than 250 words:

1. How to mend a fuse.
2. How to change a car wheel.
3. How to mend a puncture.
4. How to dial a telephone number.
5. How to make a plain cake.
6. How to make a pancake.
7. How to float in water.
8. How to tie a parcel.
9. How to cut one's toe-nails.
10. How to paper a room.

Descriptions — events

Describe carefully:

1. An interesting walk in the town or countryside.
2. A visit to the cinema you enjoyed.
3. An interesting custom you know about.
4. A holiday which was unusual.
5. An important pleasure (or business) trip you have had.
6. A journey by plane, ship or train that you have liked.
7. A television programme which you particularly enjoyed.

Descriptions — people, animals, scenes and places

Describe:

1. Your family at breakfast.
2. A teacher whom you know well.
3. Your dentist or doctor.
4. A vicar, curate or priest you know.
5. An unusual person.
6. Your best friend.
7. Your father, mother, sister or brother.
8. Any insect you know about.
9. Your favourite animal.
10. Your favourite bird.

11. Your living room.
12. The best room in your house.
13. The town, village or district where you live.
14. Your own garden.
15. Your local sports, youth or community centre.
16. Your local museum.
17. A busy airport.
18. A busy street that you know.
19. An interesting church, chapel or abbey.
20. A river, stream, reservoir or lake.

Report writing

Write a report on:

1. A sports field or complex you have visited.
2. A restaurant or cafe you know well.
3. The decoration in your own home.
4. The plumbing in your home.
5. As secretary to the Universal Bulb Company you have been invited to visit their branches in Wales, where the sales of the products have dwindled. Write a report of your findings and recommendations to the Managing Director of your Company.
6. As secretary of the Automatic Equipment Company you have been asked to look at a local site to build a new factory. Give the advantages and disadvantages of any site known to you and note your recommendations in a report to the Board.

VOCABULARY WORK

We have seen elsewhere how important vocabulary work is. This section and the next deals with further aspects. Amongst other things we shall deal with are the dictionary and its uses, words misused, overworked words, collections, the right word and simple words.

In the next section we continue our work on idiomatic English including colloquialisms and deal with slang, clichés, foreign words and phrases, American English, archaic and dialect words and words from proper names.

USING A DICTIONARY

It is necessary to have a dictionary by your side as you work in English subjects. Subjects like history, geography, social studies, commerce, economics and government will also become clearer if you keep your dictionary handy. One of the most reliable and handy dictionaries I have used is Nelson's Contemporary English Dictionary.

What help does a dictionary give?

1. It tells us how to pronounce words correctly. Most dictionaries have a 'key to pronunciation' and provided you follow this key you should be able to say the words properly. In this connection look up the words adept, condemn, indict and philosophy.

2. It tells us how to spell words. Provided you have some knowledge of the word to be spelt such as it starts with 'sc' and finishes with 'ic' you will be able to find them, e.g., scientific. Look up the following words to see that they are spelt correctly:

   Quarrelled; correspondence; disappear; inoculate; vacillate; vicissitude.

3. It tells us what part of speech a word is. This is also an aid to spelling. For instance, if you know that 'practice' is a noun and 'practise' a verb, you know the correct form in this sentence,

   I must *practise* the piano daily.

Look up the difference between

practice: practise;   advice: advise;   device: devise.

4. It tells us the variety of meanings that a particular word has in English. Thus, a calendar as a noun is a system according to which the beginning and length of the years and sub-division of the year is fixed. It is also a table showing the months, days of the week, and dates of a given year. As a noun, too, it can mean a list or register. As a verb it can mean to register in a list or to arrange, analyse and index documents. We can also distinguish the word from 'calender' which is pronounced the same way but which means among other things 'a machine in which cloth or paper is pressed under rollers for the purpose of smoothing or glazing'.

5. It tells us the derivation of words and helps us to understand the meanings of them from their roots. It also gives prefixes and suffixes from which the words are made. For instance, bicycle comes from the Latin *bio.* twice and Greek *kuklos,* a circle. Similarly, the word orchard comes from the Anglo Saxon *wort,* a herb and *geard,* a yard.

Look up pagan, pantechnicon, tweezers and yeoman.

6. It tells us (or most good dictionaries should) how the words we look up are used in idiomatic expressions. For example,

Exhibition m.e. 1. maintenance, support. 2. a pension, salary or gift. 3. an endowment at a college. 4. (med) the administration of a remedy. 5. the action of exhibiting. 6. a public display. Phrase 'to make an exhibition of oneself' (colloquialism) — to show oneself in an unfavourable aspect.

WORDS MISUSED

Many words are misused in English. Some of the most common are listed.

acknowledge   'to inform someone of' something. Write 'I acknowledge the receipt of your letter' (not 'I acknowledge your letter'. This is wrong.)

acquaint   'to make known' (not 'inform' or 'tell')

advise   'to give advice' or to 'offer counsel' (not 'to give information')

aggravate   'to make worse' (not 'to provoke' or 'to annoy')

allergic   'highly sensitive' (not a 'strong dislike')

alternative   'offering a choice between two' (should not be used for 'other')

amongst   exactly the same as 'among' — the latter is preferable

anticipate   'to foresee and take action against' (not 'expect' or 'suppose')

anxious   refers to 'somebody not easy in mind' or 'earnestly wishing for something' — it should not be used for lesser or trivial matters

appreciate   'to value something' (not 'to understand')

awful   'inspiring awe, fear, wonder or respect' — an overworked word which should be avoided except in this connection

big-headed   'conceited' but is slang — use swollen-headed or conceited

chamois   'a big, wild antelope' (not a 'shammy-leather' used to clean windows)

chronic   'gone on for a long time' (not 'severe')

definitely   'certain' — an overworked word often spelt incorrectly

demean   'to behave' (not 'to lower oneself' or 'make oneself meaner')

dogma   either an 'established principle, a doctrine, solely dependent on faith' (not 'reasoning') or 'an arrogant opinion spoken with authority'

dumb   'unable to talk' (not 'stupid' which is an Americanism)

empirical   'based on practical experience' — it has nothing to do with 'imperial' which is connected 'with empire'

enhance	'to raise the value of' or 'to make larger' — it cannot be applied to a person
exotic	'introduced' or 'coming from abroad' (not 'fascinating' or 'desirable')
extenuate	'to partly excuse'
exterminate	'to destroy completely' (not 'killing one person')
feasible	'able to be done, practicable' (cannot always be used as an alternative for 'possible' and 'probable')
feel	'to touch' (not 'think or consider')
flaunt	'to display ostentatiously' (should not be confused with 'flout' meaning 'to defy the law')
ghastly	'to terrify' — another overworked word
homo	'man' in Latin; 'the same' in Greek — be careful you know which is meant
inculcate	'to teach by repetition' — note we can only inculcate in or upon a person
individual	'single' and should not be used for a person
inimitable	'something which cannot be imitated' (not the 'one and only')
late	often used for someone who has left a position (e.g., the late headmistress — the retired headmistress) but care must be taken that it does not suggest the person is dead
learn	'to get knowledge' or 'to study' (not 'to give knowledge to someone else' — to teach)
mercurial	'changeable' or 'fickle' (should not be confused with 'murky')
meticulous	'extremely careful, unnecessarily so', — it is not a synonym for 'careful', 'exact' or 'precise'
mutual	' relationship between two persons' or things — each other (not 'common')
nice	'agreeable' — another overworked word

practically	'empirically, based on one's experience' is opposite of 'theoretically' and should not be used for 'almost'
risque	'salacious', 'almost improper' (not 'dangerous — risky')
same	'exactly similar' (not the same as 'similar' which suggests a resemblance)
scholar	'learned person who is concerned with original thought' (not the same as 'pupil' — a child who is taught at school or college)
transpire	'to become known' (not 'to happen')
utilise	'put to a useful purpose' or 'to find a use for something that might be wasted' (not a synonym for 'use')

Besides those listed there are numerous other overworked words. Some of these are fabulous, lovely, got, terrible, stupendous, literally, beastly, dreadful, gorgeous and deadly. Avoid these whenever you can.

GROUP COLLECTIVES

It is important for the student to learn certain group collective nouns, e.g., *a library of books*. The following list is not exhaustive but includes the most common the student is likely to meet.

Archipelago — islands
army — soldiers
assembly — people
association — people
audience — people

Bale — cotton, wool
band — musicians, outlaws, people, robbers
baren — mules

bench — bishops, magistrates
bevy — ladies, maidens, larks quails, roes
board — directors, governors, interviewers
body — people, soldiers
bouquet — flowers
brood — birds, chickens, ducklings, goslings

budget — papers
building — rooks
bunch — bananas, flowers,
    grapes, keys
bundle — rags, sticks

Cast — actors, hawks
caste — flower pots
catch — fish
cete — badgers
chest — drawers
choir — angels, singers
chorus — birds, singers
class — pupils, scholars
cloud — insects
clowder — cats
clump — trees
cluster — animals, diamonds
    flowers, people,
    stars
clutch — eggs
collection — pictures, stamps
company — actors, soldiers
congregation — people
    (in church)
constellation — stars
covert — coots
covey — grouse
crate — crockery, fruit
crew — sailors
crowd — people

Down — hares
drove — cattle

Fall — woodcocks
family — relations
field — runners
flight — aircraft, doves,
    birds, insects, steps,
    swallows
flock — birds, geese, people,
    sheep

forest — trees
fusilade — shots

Gaggle — geese
galaxy — stars
gang — boys, criminals,
    elks, labourers
gathering — clans, people
group — animals, islands,
    people, things

Hail — fire
hedge — bushes
herd — antelopes, buffaloes,
    cattle, cows, cranes, pigs
horde — savages
host — angels, people, sparrows

Kindle — kittens

Labour — moles
leap — leopards
library — books
litter — cubs, piglets, puppies

Menagerie — animals
mob — people (rioting)
multitude — people
muster — peacocks

Nest — birds, mice, rabbits,
    machine-guns
nide — pheasants

Orchestra — musicians

Pace — asses
pack — cards, hounds, rascals,
    wolves
paddling — ducks
panel — jurymen
party — friends, people
peal — bells

plague — insects, locusts
pride — lions
punnet — strawberries

Queue — people in a line

Race — people
rag — colts
regiment — soldiers
rope — pearls

School — porpoises, whales
set — cards, china, clubs, tools
sheaf — arrows, corn, papers
shoal — fish, herring
shock — wheat
siege — herons
skein — silk, wool
skulk — foxes
sloth — bears
smuck — jellyfish
species — animals, birds, insects, reptiles
squad — policemen, soldiers

squadron — aircraft
stack — hay
staff — servants, teachers
stand — plovers
string — beads, horses, pearls
stud — horses
suit — clothes
suite — furniture, personal servants, rooms
swarm — bees, insects, people

Team — horses, oxen, players
throng — people
tribe — goats, natives, people
troop — horsemen, lions, monkeys, scouts, soldiers
troupe — dancers, minstrels
truss — hay
tuft — grass

Watch — nightingales
wisp — snipe

DIFFERENCES BETWEEN WORDS

Below are fifty sets of words which are often confused.

Adjacent	lying close
contiguous	so close as to be touching
admission	to allow in (informal)
admittance	having permission or right to enter (formal)
adventitious	accidental, casual
adventurous	enterprising, risk-taking
aesthetic	concerned with beauty and art
ascetic	self denial
Arctic	North Pole
Antarctic	South Pole
atheist	a person who denies the existence of God
agnostic	a person who is not sure whether God exists or not
while	for a short time
a while	a period of time (may be long or short)
beside	alongside, next to
besides	in addition to, as well as
biannual	half yearly
biennial	every two years
biography	a person's life story written by someone else
autobiography	a person's life story written by himself (or herself)
bibliography	a list of works (books consulted)
by	near, at, beside
bye	subordinate, incidental
canon	a rule or standard, relating to the church
cannon	a gun
carat	weight of a precious stone
carrot	a vegetable
caret	sign used in writing and proof reading to show an addition to a text
childish	behaving like a child, immature, puerile, silly
childlike	simple, innocent

concave	hollowed out like the inside of a circle or sphere
convex	curving like the outside of a circle or sphere
construct	to build
construe	to deduce, interpret
contemptible	deserving contempt
contemptuous	showing or expressing contempt
definite	clear, precise
definitive	last, final, unequivocal
diminish	to make less, to become less
minimize	to estimate at a minimum
equable	regular, without variation
equitable	fair, reasonable
exceptional	unusual, strange
exceptionable	objectionable
explicit	expressed clearly
implicit	implied, not spoken
forego	to go before, precede
forgo	to go without, to deny oneself
gourmand	a greedy eater
gourmet	a person who eats with discrimination, a connoisseur
honorary	an honour given without payment
honourable	worthy of respect, high-minded, honest
hypercritical	being too severe, too critical
hypocritical	acting dishonestly, a pretender
imperial	supreme, majestic, relating to empire
imperious	arrogant, domineering
instructional	educational
instructive	informative
inveigh	speak against violently
inveigle	to entice, to persuade
lifelong	lasting throughout life
livelong	whole, entire

misogamist	a person who hates marriage
misogynist	a person who hates women
moral	lesson, point in a story
morale	general spirit, *camaraderie, ésprit de corps,* discipline
morals	general principles
obsequial	relating to a funeral
obsequious	compliant, too eager to please
observance	keeping a duty or custom
observation	keeping watch, noticing things
obsolete	out of date
obsolescent	to be going out of date
oculist	a person who treats eye diseases
optician	a person who makes and sells optical instruments especially spectacles
practicable	can be done or accomplished
practical	suitable for particular circumstances
peninsula	a piece of land almost surrounded by water
peninsular	resembling a peninsula
poser	a question difficult to answer, a person who poses for a portrait or photograph
poseur	a person who behaves affectedly in order to impress
presumptive	probable, presumed
presumptious	over-confident, arrogant
pseudonym	pen-name adopted by a writer
alias	a name assumed by someone to conceal his real identity
incognito	an important person travelling in an assumed name to disguise his identity
nom de plume	pen-name (pseudonym)
review	a survey, a re-examination, a publication, an inspection of troops
revue	stage entertainment
sentiment	sympathy
sentimentality	excessive display of emotion

slander	false words about people — spoken
libel	false words about people — written
summon	to send for
summons	an order to appear in court
therefor	for this, for that or for it
therefore	for that reason
thrash	corporal punishment (beating a person)
thresh	beating grain
virtual	in effect but not in reality
virtuous	pure in mind and deed
weird	supernatural
weary	tired

SIMPLE WORDS

When writing English, it is always best to use the ordinary, common-place, Anglo-Saxon word. Write simple direct English. Thus, a *lie* is a *lie* not a *terminological inexactitude.* The following is a list of words and phrases for which simpler words can be used.

Word or Phrase	**Meaning**
Nuptial ceremony	wedding
adverse climatic conditions	bad weather
a pyrotechnic display	fireworks
deliberate intrepidity	cool courage
a caudal appendage	a tail
a chef d'oeuvre	a masterpiece
an initial endeavour	a start
evinced	showed
perturbation	anxiety
a multitudinous assemblage	many people

WORDS INSTEAD OF PHRASES, CLAUSES OR SENTENCES

The facility to substitute a single word for a phrase, clause or even a whole sentence is essential in summary work. Your ability to do this also indicates the extent of your vocabulary. The following phrases, clauses and sentences have been replaced by single words for you.

One who takes a leading part in a struggle — *protaganist* .
A word similar in meaning to another — *synonym*.
Only for the time being — *temporary*.
Can live on land and in water — *amphibious*.
Impossible to satisfy — *insatiable*.
Capable of being interpreted in two different ways — *ambiguous*.
Able to work equally well with both hands — *ambidextrous*.
Impossible to put into practice — *impracticable*.
Goes up and down from day to day — *fluctuates*.
No law or order — *anarchy*.
Loss of feeling — *numbness*.
A plant which flowers year after year — *perennial*.
A house not fit to live in — *inhabitable*.
One who publishes a collection of literary passages — *publisher*.
One who looks on the bright side of life — *optimist*.
One who looks on the bad side of life — *pessimist*.
A group of stars — *galaxy*.
A dog of mixed breed — *mongrel*.
A conversation between two people — *dialogue*.
A man talking to himself aloud — *soliloquy*.
A five sided figure — *pentagon*.
Trivial and commonplace — *trite*.
Of enormous dimensions — *huge*.
Prejudiced in favour of one side or party — *biased*.
Impossible to calculate — *incalculable*.
Obstinately sticking to a creed or opinion — *bigoted*.
A writer of another's life-story — *biographer*.
Collective slaughter of men in battle — *massacre*.
The killing of oneself — *suicide*.
Killing one's own father (mother) — *patricide (matricide)*.
A letter or certificate of recommendation — *testimonial*.
Place at school or college where meals are served — *refectory*.

One belonging to the same country as oneself — *compatriot*.
An addition to a will — *codicil*.
Conformity to established rules and customs, especially of behaviour — *etiquette*.
Handed down from one person to another — *bequeathed*.
Occurring every three years — *triennially*.
Inclined to be fat — *corpulent*.
Contrary to law — *illegal*.
In a condition between childhood and manhood — *teenager*.
Trained by practice, skilled — *expert*.
Send out (commodities) from one country to another — *export*.
Put out, quench — *extinguish*.

WORDS SIMILAR IN SOUND

Below is a list of some of the most common words which sound the same:

Air, heir
aisle, isle, I'll
alley, ally
allowed, aloud
ant, aunt
assent, ascent
ate, eight
awl, all

Bad, bade
bail, bale
bald, bawled
ball, bawl
bare, bear
beach, beech
bell, belle
blew, blue
boar, bore
board, bored
boy, buoy
braid, brayed
bridal, bridle
buy, by, bye

Ceiling, scaling
cellar, seller
cereal, serial
cheap, cheep
check, cheque
choir, quire
coarse, course
coat, cote
colonel, kernel
compliment, complement
cord, chord
core, corps
council, counsel
councillor, counsellor
crews, cruise
current, currant

Dear, deer
desert, dessert
die, dye
draft, draught

Ewe, you, yew

Faint, feint
fair, fare
feat, feet
flour, flower
flue, flew
fore, four
frays, phrase

Gait, gate
gamble, gambol
great, grate
groan, grown
guilt, gilt

Hail, hale
hair, hare
hear, here
heard, herd
higher, hire
him, hymn
hole, whole
holy, wholly
horde, hoard
hour, our

Key, quay
knead, need
knew, new
knight, night
knot, not
knows, nose

Leak, leek
lightening, lightning
lone, loan
lute, loot

Maid, made
male, mail
mane, main
meddle, medal
meet, meat, mete

mist, missed
mussel, muscle

Nun, none

Oar, ore, o'er

Pair, pear, pare
pale, pail
pane, pain
pause, paws
peal, peel
peer, pier
picture, pitcher
piece, peace
place, plaice
plain, plane
plum, plumb
pores, pours
principal, principle
profit, prophet

Queue, cue

Rain, reign
raise, raze, rays
read, reed
real, reel
reek, wreak
right, rite, wright, write
ring, wring
road, rowed, rode
root, route
rose, rows
rye, wry

Sail, sale
scene, seen
scent, sent, cent
sea, see
seam, seem
sew, sow, so
sight, site

sole, soul
son, sun
stair, stare
stake, steak
stationary, stationery
steal, steel
stile, style
story, storey

Tail, tale
tares, tears
tears, tiers
their, there
threw, through

throne, thrown
tide, tied
time, thyme
to, too, two
told, tolled

Vain, vane, vein
vale, veil

Waist, waste
wait, weight
weak, week
won, one,
wood, would

Yolk, yoke

PRACTICE QUESTIONS

Overworked Words

1. Get and got

    Rewrite the following without using 'get' or 'got'.

    (i) Have you *got* the records?

    (ii) I have *got* to go now.

    (iii) They have just *got* a house.

    (iv) I wonder when we shall *get* home.

    (v) "*Get* your mackintosh, it's raining," he said.

2. Nice

    Rewrite the following without using the word 'nice'.

    (i) She is such a *nice* lady.

    (ii) You are in a *nice* predicament now.

    (iii) It is *nice* and cool in here.

(iv) That is a *nice* remark to make.

(v) The grandfather was a *nice* old man.

3.   Quite

Rewrite the following without using the word 'quite'.

(i) We have eaten *quite* a lot today.

(ii) The crooner sang *quite* a good song.

(iii) Don't fret yourself, I shall be *quite* alright.

(iv) We have had *quite* a good time today.

(v) Don't you agree with me? (Answer) *Quite*.

4.   Distinguish between the following sets of words:

(i) Addicted
    devoted
	(ii) adverse
	    averse
		(iii) artful
		    artless

(iv) careless
    carefree
	(v) character
	    reputation
		(vi) classic
		    classics
		    classical

(vii) considerable
    considerate
	(viii) contagious
	    contiguous
		(ix) credible
		    creditable

(x) deprecate
    depreciate
	(xi) discomfit
	    discomfort
		(xii) distinct
		    distinctive

(xiii) eatable
    edible
	(xiv) effective
	    efficient
	    efficacious
		(xv) entrant
		    entry

(xvi) extended
    extensive
	(xvii) favourable
	    favourite
		(xviii) glance
		    glimpse

(xix) honorary
    honourable
	(xx) imaginary
	    imaginative	

5.   Distinguish between the following sets of words:

(i) Infer
    imply
	(ii) ingenious
	    ingenuous
		(iii) Jacobean
		    Jacobite

(iv) laudable
    laudatory

(v) masterful
    mastery

(vi) perceive
    conceive

(vii) pitiable
    pitiful

(viii) potent
    potential

(ix) relative
    relevant

(x) sensual
    sensuous

(xi) specially
    especially

(xii) sty
    stye

(xiii) swat
    swot

(xiv) titillate
    titivate

(xv) tortious
    tortuous
    torturous

(xvi) triumphant
    triumphal

(xvii) vicious
    viscous

(xviii) wrapped
    rapt

(xix) candid
    candied

(xx) introvert
    extrovert

6.   Give adjectives ending in -al for each of the following phrases:

  (i) Trivial and commonplace

 (ii) of married life

(iii) pertaining to a current subject of discussion

(iv) lasting for a short time only

 (v) equally skilled in two languages

(vi) a tendency to act in a certain way

(vii) lasting or continuing for a number of years

(viii) performed in one day

 (ix) occurring during the night

  (x) lasting for ever

 (xi) belonging to a father

(xii) pertaining to the soul

(xiii) pertaining to the body

(xiv) pertaining to spring

 (xv) intermittently going on

(xvi) lasting for two years

(xvii) pertaining to a bride or worn by a bride

(xviii) very thrifty or saving

(xix) having the disposition or temper of an enemy

(xx) shaped like a cone

(xxi) exactly the same

(xxii) relating to the base or ground work of something

(xxiii) pertaining to the four elements or any one of them

(xxiv) causing loss or danger

(xxv) belonging to or situated in the East (West)

7. **Show how** each of the following words can be used to express different meanings (homonyms):

down, canon, bill, corn, charger, leaves.

8. **Give a single noun** for each of the following:

(i) A many-sided geometrical figure

(ii) a five-sided geometrical figure

(iii) an instrument that magnifies minute objects

(iv) an instrument that measures heat and cold

(v) a device that indicates the weather

(vi) a machine that takes photographs through the body

(vii) a device that tells if an object is horizontal

(viii) a device that tells if an object is vertical

(ix) an instrument which makes electricity

(x) a ship's engine which works by steam

(xi) a device for measuring angles in surveying

(xii) a device which helps the voice to carry

(xiii) an instrument which carries sound without using wires

(xiv) a device which indicates direction

(xv) a device which causes the spark in an engine

9. **Choose the** correct word in each of the following:

   (i) We are not (aloud, allowed) to speak during a church sermon.

   (ii) He will give us no (piece, peace) until we give him another (peace, piece) of apple tart.

   (iii) The conductor paid us some very pretty (complements, compliments) after our performance.

   (iv) Jane did not (practice, practise) the piano very long this morning.

   (v) Before us, we saw a very (precipitate, precipitous) path.

10. **The following** sentences all contain examples of words wrongly used. Correct them by substituting the correct words.

    (i) John is a most aggravating person.

    (ii) We noticed a very strange-looking individual approaching our car.

    (iii) The popular music was so loud that it literally raised the roof.

    (iv) Harry is a mutual friend of Tom and Joe.

    (v) Mary told us what transpired at the meeting.

11. **The following** sentences contain unnecessary words. Rewrite each sentence using fewer and simpler words where possible.

    (i) The girl said she liked the present equally as well as the other.

    (ii) Pigeons in great numbers abound on these islands.

    (iii) We shall be delighted to act in mutual co-operation with you.

    (iv) An extremely unique feature of the variety programme is the low number of people used in it which are are not very many.

    (v) He recovered rapidly from his illness and is now quite better.

    (vi) The two 'buses collided together at great speed.

    (vii) The orchestra was quite inaudible and could not be heard by anyone.

    (viii) I was seated all alone by myself in the corner.

    (ix) The general resigned from his post.

    (x) In the event of your agreeing, we will send it at once.

STYLES OF WRITING
AND LANGUAGE

SLANG, COLLOQUIALISM, CLICHÉ AND IDIOM

Let us first look at the styles of writing which people use to express themselves and in so doing consider some technical terms which we should know.

1. **Colloquial writing** is informal and describes writing which uses words used in common speech.

2. **Journalese** is the kind of writing used by newspaper reporters and other journalists.

3. **Johnsonese** is the kind of writing full of long words which come from the classics (Latin and Greek).

4. **Commercialese** is the kind of writing found in letters. It is really business and commercial language.

5. **Purple passages** are pieces of prose (kinds of writing) in which the writer has done his best to use every technique he knows about. He tries to get his message over by using sonorous phrases, similes and metaphors and attempts to be profound and poetic, eloquent and sonorous all in the same passage.

Generally speaking, the student writer should avoid all the styles of writing mentioned above. All these styles involve the use of the following, generally regarded as things to be avoided in written work.

Slang

Slang refers to spoken words which are frowned upon in polite conversation as well as in written work, e.g.,

STANDARD ENGLISH	COLLOQUIAL ENGLISH	SLANG ENGLISH
man	chap	bloke
young woman	girl	bird
mad	off his head	round the bend
friend	pal	mate
fool	idiot	dummy

Cliché

Cliché refers to expressions or phrases which are used over and over again. These have been used so often that they lack interest and are stale and automatic. A few examples are listed below:

as hard as nails
to get down to brass tacks
filthy lucre
the inner man
this day and age
the man in the street
the generation gap
the wind of change
our fine feathered friends
the inflationary spiral

the fair sex
too funny for words
young hopefuls
tender mercies
at the parting of the ways
the psychological moment
sleeping the sleep of the just
the rising generation
the energy gap

There are so many clichés in the language that it is impossible to list them all but a selection appears later.

Jargon

Jargon refers to the type of speech used by a small group of people. It may be those belonging to a particular sect, religion, trade, science, art, profession or political party. The words used are often unintelligible to those outside the particular group. Examples of jargon are:

neutralisation; double decomposition; ionic; electrolysis; reduction; displacement; efflorescence; sequestered; isomerism; discharge.

SOME SLANG WORDS AND CLICHÉS EXPLAINED

Below is a short list of slang and clichés, most of which one can hear in everyday conversation. The student should remember that these change as the language changes and often words that our forebearers called slang have become acceptable. Also, it is difficult to decide when a particular saying or phrase becomes a cliché.

Slang word or phrase	Meaning
A. 1.	first class
Adam's ale	water
hot air	empty talk
all for it	completely in favour
all in	completely exhausted
all my eye	nonsense
all of a tiswas	very agitated/confused
all set	ready and willing
all the rage	fashionable
anchors	brakes
and how!	I do agree!
have ants in one's pants	be very excited
are you fit?	are you ready?
argy-bargy	dispute
as sure as eggs	very certain
ask me another!	I do not know
at a loose end	temporarily with nothing to do
at a pinch	in an emergency
back-chat	impudent reply
the back of beyond	somewhere remote
fed up to the back teeth	bored
bad egg	untrustworthy person
a bad show	unfortunate
baddie	villain
half-baked	muddled
bamboozle	swindle

Slang word or phrase	Meaning
bang on	very accurate
bank on	rely on
barney	quarrel
like a bat out of hell	very quickly
on one's beam-ends	worn out, short of cash
beatnik	drop-out
beddy-byes	sleep
all beer and skittles	extremely pleasant
bellyful	enough
belt up	be quiet
best bib and tucker	best clothes
better half	wife
bit soft Nellie	idiot
bilge	nonsense
bleed like a (stuck) pig	bleed profusely
blood-wagon	ambulance
bloomer	mistake
blue-eyed boy	favourite
boloney	nonsense
bone idle	very lazy
bonkers	mad
bread and butter	livelihood
brew up	make tea
bubbly	Champagne
go for a burton	vanish
cabbage-head	simpleton
in the cart	in trouble
hard cheese	bad luck
chinwag	gossip
a cinch	a certainty
codswallop	nonsense
come clean	confess
croak	die
cuppa	cup of tea
cushy	easy, pleasant
dead on	accurate
flashy	showy
fork out	pay
fuzz	police
blow the gaff	reveal a secret
gasper	cigarette

Slang word or phrase	Meaning
gen	news, information
glad rags	smart clothes
go places	travel
gravy	money
grub	food
up a gum-tree	in difficulty
half-slewed	half drunk
old hand	experienced person
hokey	prison
hoo-ha	fuss
hot air	empty talk
hot water	in trouble, disgrace
hubby	husband
hunky-dory	very pleasing
in the pink	in good health
iron out	solve
have an itching palm	greed for money
have itchy feet	ambitious for promotion (or travel)
Jock	Scotsman
junkie	drug addict
just the job	exactly what is required
knock about	wander
knock spots off	be superior to
korky	idiotic, strange
lashings	lots
level pegging	keeping abreast
lie-in	sleep longer than usual
lolly	money (as is Triviato lollipop)
low-down	information
dead-pan	without any expression
digs	lodgings
dog-end	cigarette end
doorstep	very thick sandwich
in easy street	very comfortably off
elbow grease	physical effort
up to one's eyes	very busy
fall-guy	scapegoat
falling off a log	easy
flaked out	exhausted
make one's pile	acquire wealth

Slang word or phrase	Meaning
mingy	mean
moke	donkey
murphy	potato
mushy	sentimental
niggly	irritable
noddle	head
not on your nelly	certainly not
nuts and bolts	essentials, basics
off the cuff	without prior preparation
off the record	not for disclosure
once in a blue moon	very rarely
out in the cold	isolated, cut off
own up	confess
paper over the cracks	conceal deficiencies
pea-souper	dense fog
pen-pusher	clerk
pony	£25
pricey	expensive
put the screws on	force
queer one's pitch	spoil one's chances
pop the question	propose marriage
rat-trap	mouth
rough stuff	rough behaviour
run-down	unwell
run the tape over	examine
sarny	sandwich
shambles	confusion
shenannicking	trickery
the shove	termination of employment
side-kick	helper, assistant
skint	without money
so-so	fairly well
in the soup	in difficulty
stoke up	eat
sweeten	bribe
tich	small person
togs	clothes
turf out	eject
twaddle	nonsense
twit	fool
undies	underwear

Slang	Meaning
on the up and up	improving
up tight	very tense
slow on the uptake	dim-witted
vamoose	leave
villain	criminal
wallah	person
well-heeled	wealthy
whizz-kid	lively, progressive, intelligent, successful young person
wipe the floor with	reprimand
wizard	splendid
write-up	newspaper review or article
yap	talk too much
yobbo	lout
yummy	attractive
zero hour	time to begin

Colloquialism	Meaning
ad-lib	improvise
catch one's death	get a severe chill
like a Cheshire cat	smiling broadly with satisfaction
clean as a whistle	absolutely clean
cloak and dagger	secret
cock a snook	show contempt or derision
get cold feet	become afraid
cook the books	falsify the accounts
cook one's goose	destroy someone; place someone in great difficulty
cramp one's style	handicap someone
cut a figure	make an impression
devil-may-care	reckless
dog bites dog	like criticizes like
donkey's years	for a long time
down in the dumps	depressed
dull as ditch water	very dull, stupid, very uninteresting
a fair crack of the whip	a fair deal
fit as a fiddle	in good health
French leave	departure or absence without permission
full of beans	in good health
a gentleman of fortune	a criminal
get it in the neck	be punished
get off on the wrong foot	start badly
get off one's chest	relieve one's feelings of anxiety or guilt by disclosing something
a gold-mine	a profitable business
like greased lightning	very quickly
give a big hand to	applaud loudly
have a heart	be merciful
heart-to-heart	frank, intimate conversation
show a clean pair of heels	run away quickly
in full swing	fully working and successful
jump down one's throat	criticize or scold severely
jump out of one's skin	be very startled
jump the gun	be premature

Colloquialism	Meaning
dead beat	exhausted
in the same boat	in similar circumstances
down in the mouth	dejected
down on one's luck	having some misfortune
all ears	paying close attention
at a loose end	nothing to do
good for nothing	useless
hard of hearing	almost deaf
hard up	short of money
hard hit	in serious trouble
lion-hearted	having great courage
at loggerheads	quarrelling
the man in the street	an ordinary person
an old salt	an experienced sailor
at rest	dead
out of sorts	ill
stuck up	proud and conceited
beside oneself	annoyed
heavy-eyed	sleepy
sweep the board	win everything
draw the long bow	tell unbelievable stories
make a clean breast of	confess
throw in the towel throw in the sponge }	give in
show a clean pair of heels	escape
lead a dog's life	having a wretched existence
draw the line	fix the limit
keep one's powder dry	be prepared
make both ends meet	manage financially
get into hot water	get into trouble
just one of those things	something which happens that has to be accepted
keen as mustard	very eager
keep one's head above water	managing to survive although in difficulties
keep one's eyes peeled	remain alert
keep under one's hat	keep secret
kick up a row	cause a disturbance
to knuckle down	to begin an unpleasant task

Colloquialism	Meaning
the last straw	the final event (in a series) which causes collapse
swing the lead	avoid work
not to lift one's little finger	not to make the slightest effort
live like a lord	live in luxury
meet one's Waterloo	encounter final defeat
miss the boat	to be too late
all the more the merrier	the greater the number, the better it will be
a near miss	nearly a hit
no laughing matter	a serious affair
not worth the paper it's written on	worthless
nothing to write home about	insignificant
old-hat	out of date
on one's toes	alert
on top of the world	elated
once in a blue moon	very rarely
other pebbles on the beach	alternative opportunities possible
out of commission	not functioning
out of the ordinary	unusual
overstep the mark	exceed accepted limits
play the game	to be fair
hit below the belt	act unfairly
pull one's leg	to tease
hold one's tongue	keep quiet
hit the nail on the head	to be accurate
tell it to the Marines	to disbelieve
sling mud	to defame
go through the mill	to suffer
nip in the bud	to stop something
put the cart before the horse	to do something the wrong way round
to rain cats and dogs	to rain heavily
raise one's dander	to become angry
take a rise out of	to deceive
turn the tables	reverse a result
let the cat out of the bag	to disclose a secret
act the goat	behave foolishly

Colloquialism	Meaning
swing the lead	to shun working
haul over the coals	to scold or punish
chew the fat	to talk or argue
take forty winks	a short nap
turn up one's nose	to ignore
showing the white feather	being a coward
the green-eyed monster	jealousy
as the crow flies	direct
show one's paces	show one's abilities
pass out	to faint
keep one's pecker up	be cheerful (especially in adversity)
the penny has dropped	the point has been understood
pick a bone	quarrel
give a piece of one's mind	scold
make a pig's ear	make a mess
pipped at the post	narrowly beaten
plain as the nose on one's face	very obvious
play for safety	take no risks
play the game	follow accepted rules
pluck someone's goose	humiliate someone
pretty penny	large sum of money
pull a fast one	take advantage
push up the daisies	to be dead
put in the picture	inform
put paid to	defeat
put the wind up	frighten
put years on somebody	shorten one's life
put it right there	shake hands
rock the boat	make things difficult for others
go round in circles	be active without result
rush-job	something that has to be finished quickly
scratch along	manage to live
see how the land lies	to find out what the position is

Cliché	Meaning
accidents will happen	mishaps will occur
ace up one's sleeve	to have something in reserve
act in cold blood	to do an evil deed deliberately
an admirable Crichton	a person extremely good at many things, an all-rounder
all the world and his wife	everybody
the almighty Dollar	the power of wealth
the apple of discord	a source of contention
at daggers drawn	hostile to each other
at one fell swoop	at one blow
at the psychological moment	at the critical time
to have no axe to grind	without private motive or grievance
bag and baggage	completely
battle-royal	a free-for-all fight
be in the same boat	to be in the same situation
be that as it may	nevertheless
have a bee in one's bonnet	to be obsessed by something
bete-noire	a bugbear
one's better half	one's wife
beyond the pale	beyond the bounds of decency
blessing in disguise	good coming from evil
blue-blood	aristocratic ancestors
born and bred	a native of
born with a silver spoon in one's mouth	born lucky (or wealthy)
a brown study	a very sad, serious person
to look as if butter would not melt in one's mouth	to appear innocent
by hook or by crook	to use any means to achieve one's purpose
call a spade a spade	to speak with unusual frankness
captains of industry	executives controlling big business
castles in the air (also castles in Spain)	false imaginings of a rosy future
caviare to the general	something which ordinary people cannot appreciate

Cliché	Meaning
the city fathers	town councillors
to consign to oblivion	to forget completely
consummation devoutly to be wished	an extremely desirable result
crocodile tears	feigning weeping, false sympathy
to damn with faint praise	to condemn something by hardly praising it at all
depart this life	to die
die in harness	to expire while still working
the die is cast	the decision has been irrevocably made
to draw the long bow	to exaggerate greatly
to drop the pilot	to dismiss
eager for the fray	keen to fight
at the eleventh hour	at the last minute
fall between two stools	to fail because of hesitation between alternatives
he first saw the light of day	he was born
flesh and blood	human nature, a relative
foregone conclusion	the end already known
from pillar to post	ceaselessly
to go the whole hog	to make every effort despite the cost
the golden mean	the ideal average
good for nothing	worthless
good in parts	of mixed character
a good samaritan	a person who helps others in distress
goods and chattels	personal property
to grasp the nettle	to tackle a difficult situation boldly
a great ovation	much applause
to hang on like grim death	to hold very tightly
bound hand and foot	completely controlled
to be hand in glove	to work well with someone
the happy pair	a bridal couple
have too many irons in the fire	involved in too much
to have a heart of gold	to be very kind-hearted
hell for leather	at great speed

Cliché	Meaning
helping hand	giving assistance
hewers of wood and drawers of water	humble workers or labourers
hit the nail on the head	to guess or state correctly
I am not my brother's keeper	not morally responsible for a person
the idle rich	wealthy people who do not work
in a cleft stick	in a serious dilemma
in apple-pie order	extremely tidy
in round numbers	approximately
in the arms of Morpheus	asleep
in the public eye	prominent
in the same boat	in similar circumstances
jumping-off point	starting place
keep the pot boiling	earn enough to live on
kill the fatted calf	to celebrate (usually someone's return)
to speak the King's English	to speak English accurately
to know the ropes	to be well-informed
leave to one's own devices	to be left alone
to shed light on the subject	to make something clear
the lion's share	the largest part
lock, stock and barrel	completely, entirely
make a mountain out of a molehill	to exaggerate
man in the street	an ordinary citizen
a mare's nest	a disappointment, something worthless
matter of life and death	something extremely important
much of a muchness	very much alike
their name is legion	very numerous
nine days' wonder	exciting news which is soon forgotten
to nip in the bud	to put a stop to something
not to put too fine a point upon it	to speak bluntly
to hold out an olive branch	to propose peace
on pins and needles	extremely uneasy
to be on tenterhooks	to be in suspense or impatient

Cliché	Meaning
once and for all	finally
part and parcel	an essential portion
to pay the piper and call the tune	to pay the expenses and to say what is to be done
to pick up the threads	to resume a piece of work
to play the game	to act honourably
to plough the sands	to engage in fruitless work
the powers that be	those in authority
a queer fish	a strange person
it is quite providential	very lucky
the root of all evil	money
to run to seed	to degenerate
to be in sackcloth and ashes	to be penitent or grief stricken
not to say boo to a goose	too timid to speak
to set one's teeth	to be determined
ships that pass in the night	persons who meet and pass on unlikely to meet again
shipshape and Bristol fashion	orderly
the sinews of war	money
a sorry jest	a pointless joke
spick and span	very neat
the staff of life	bread
step by step	slow, regular progress
storm in a tea-cup	great fuss about a trifle
a swan-song	a final talk, speech or count
to take a leaf out of someone's book	to imitate
to tell tales out of school	to betray secrets
to be thankful for small mercies	to be grateful for little things
this vale of tears	the world
to throw down the glove	to issue a challenge
to have one's tongue in one's cheek	to speak without sincerity
a tower of strength	a powerful or reliable person
true blue	staunch unwavering principles (especially Tory)
the turn of the tide	change in fortune
to twist round one's little finger	to have someone completely under one's influence

Cliché	Meaning
to be under a cloud	to be in disgrace
to upset the apple-cart	to spoil a plan or intention
a vexed question	a difficult decision
a virgin page	an empty page (i.e. not written on)
to wear the trousers	a woman who dominates her husband
to wend one's way	to go
to win golden opinions	to be well received
the witching hour	midnight
a woman's glory	the (long) hair of a woman
woman's intuition	a woman's ability to guess correctly
the writing on the wall	an event or incident that shows bad luck or ill fortune to come
at your earliest convenience	as soon as you can

IDIOMS

We must now turn to idiom. An idiom is a form of expression or a phrase which is peculiar to a particular language. Put another way an idiom is the use of familiar words in an unfamiliar sense. There are four main types of idiom in English.

1. Almost any noun, some verbs and pronouns can be used as adjectives — *hockey* team, *popular* press, *summer* nights.

2. Grammatical errors that have become acceptable as standard English, e.g.,

    It's me. (It is I.)

    Who are you going with? (With whom are you going?)

3. Usages which must be followed by certain prepositions and/or conjunctions, e.g.,

    anxious about; different from

4. Metaphorical expressions such as 'by leaps and bounds', 'pull one's leg' and 'burn the midnight oil'.

Here we are concerned with idioms as used in (4) above. Often metaphorical idiom, colloquialism, cliché or slang, are practically synonymous. Thus, a cliché might be an idiom which has lost its force because it has been used time and again — it has become an overworked phrase — it is an idiom yet a cliché (in this book, or in any English manual, the particular phrase could appear under the heading cliché or idiom, both would be correct).

Again, a colloquialism is an expression which is used in everyday conversation. Such an expression, even if not an idiom at first, might become an idiom in the future. Thus, such a colloquial phrase could appear under the heading of colloquialisms, clichés or idioms.

Slang refers to new and lively expressions introduced into the language. Used by young people at first and then introduced into ordinary speech, slang often develops into idioms. Thus, like the others, slang, colloquial phrases, clichés or idioms could appear under the same heading according to taste.

Idioms used metaphorically must be committed to memory by foreigners and native English speakers are expected to have a working knowledge of those used in writing and conversation. With such idiomatic expressions there are a few problems. First, an idiom should not be interpreted literally. For example, 'ring the changes' could mean

(i) ring the various combinations that are possible in A peal of bells (literal) *or*

(ii) change repeatedly from one to another of a series of Things, (metaphorical)

Similarly, care must be taken not to use literally what has become an idiom, e.g.,

Enjoying ourselves in the bathing pool we were all in the swim.

In this sentence 'in the swim' could mean literally that those in the pool were all swimming. However, 'in the swim' is an idiom with the metaphorical meaning of being 'fully involved in what is going on'. Care must be taken not to use such expressions which can cause error and ambiguity.

Lastly, care must be taken over every word of each idiom.

Any change of word even a preposition or a conjunction can alter the meaning, e.g.,

The old lady turned *the deaf ear* to our protests.

This suggests that the old lady's hearing was defective. The correct idiom is:

The old lady turned *a deaf ear* to our protests.

This means that the old lady purposely avoided listening to us.

Some common idioms, with their meanings are:

Idiom	Meaning
above board	honest
with one accord	unanimously
of no account	valueless
within an ace	very near to
an acquired taste	a taste for something unusual obtained gradually
not known from Adam	completely unknown
on all fours	on one's hands and knees
all set	fully prepared
a babe in arms	a child too young to walk
reduce to ashes	completely destroy by fire
leave no avenue unexplored	make every possible enquiry
back up	give support to
behind one's back	to do things deceitfully especially during someone's absence
bring home the bacon	to succeed in a venture
bag and baggage	luggage
bald as a coot	absolutely bald
have the ball in one's court	be responsible for the next move
strike a bargain	reach an agreement
on one's beam ends	in desperate plight especially financially
beard the lion in his den	confront an enemy or opponent openly on his own territory when in disagreement

Idiom	Meaning
dead beat	completely exhausted
bed of roses	a state of ease and luxury
hit below the belt	attack unfairly
best bib and tucker	best clothes
to blind with science	to confuse by using expert knowledge
one's blood runs cold	extreme terror or disappointment
at first blush	at first sight
feel in one's bones	to be quite sure
brain wave	sudden inspiration or plan
make a clean breast of	to confess
come down like a ton of bricks	to blame someone severely
brush up	revise
burn one's fingers	suffer because of rashness or interference
bury the hatchet	forget past quarrels
mean business	intend to take positive action
cakes and ale	having a very happy time
carry the can	be blamed
go cap in hand	seek something humbly
on the cards	likely to happen
in the cart	in danger, difficulty or disgrace
cat and dog's life	existence continually quarrelling and fighting
rain cats and dogs	very heavy rain
chicken-hearted	cowardly
clear as crystal	patently obvious
clip the wings	limit someone's power or authority
close shave	a narrow escape
cook one's goose	create problems for somebody
cry stinking fish	speak unfavourably about one's own family, trade or profession
cry wolf	cause problems by spreading false information
cut short	end abruptly
Darby and Joan	an aged and devoted husband and wife
in the dark	in ignorance
Davy Jones' locker	the sea-bed
go to the dogs	abandon all one's standards

Idiom	Meaning
draw a blank	have no success
down in the dumps (the mouth or in the doldrums)	very sad and depressed
dyed in the wood	indelibly ingrained
to have an edge on one's appetite	to be hungry
at a loose end	unoccupied
go off the deep end	become angry suddenly
have an eye to the main chance	be ready and keen to make personal profit
up to the eyes	completely occupied with something
lose face	suffer humiliation
fair-weather friend	one who befriends another only in times of success or prosperity
tickle one's fancy	to amuse or attract
fifty-fifty	to take equal shares
all fingers and thumbs	to be awkward or clumsy
flash in the pan	a brief display producing no useful result
fly off at a tangent	to abruptly change from one subject to another
a fool's paradise	a state of bliss when the facts do not merit happiness
to have feet of clay	to be weak and liable to be overthrown
fly by night	unreliable person
fork out	to pay
to blow the gaff	to reveal a secret
take up the gauntlet	to accept a challenge
go-between	an arbitrator
go through fire and water	make any sacrifice
grease a person's palm	to bribe someone
big guns (wheels)	important, influential people
all hands to the pumps	everyone should help
show one's hand	reveal one's intentions
have one's head screwed on the right way	to be shrewd
make headway	make progress

Idiom	Meaning
wear one's heart on one's sleeve	to be open and frank
kick one's heels	to waste time
high and dry	stranded
hook, line and sinker	completely and utterly
every inch	completely
ins-and-outs	the details
strike while the iron is hot	act promptly
view with a jaundiced eye	regard with envy or jealousy
jog a person's memory	remind someone about something
keep at arm's length	avoid being too familiar with
keep one's hand in	continue to practise to retain one's skill
kick up a fuss	cause a disturbance or quarrel
next of kin	nearest relations
knock into a cocked hat	defeat easily
knuckle under	to give in
like a lamb	without resisting
look to one's laurels	beware of losing one's position
lay on thick	to exaggerate
lead a dance	cause anxiety
lead up the garden path	to deceive
let one's hair down	to relax completely
light upon	to discover by chance
lock, stock and barrel	entirely
a lump in one's throat	feeling sympathy or pity for someone
mad as a March hare	completely insane
make it up	become friendly again after quarrelling
a man of straw	a worthless person
wide of the mark	very inaccurate
a square meal	a full meal
on one's mettle	roused to do one's best
milk-and-water	feeble, weak
pin-money	money supplied for small pleasures and amusements
month of Sundays	a long, indefinite time

Idiom	Meaning
make one's mouth water	create a sense of pleasant anticipation
keen as mustard	very eager
nail one's colours to the mast	to demonstrate one's allegiance publicly
on the nail	immediately, promptly
get it in the neck	be scolded or punished
a hard nut to crack	a difficult person or problem to deal with
in a nutshell	summarised briefly
in bad odour	unpopular
once in a blue moon	very rarely
the order of the day	the current fashion
overshoot the mark	to go too far
own up	to confess
keep pace	to maintain the same speed
hold one's peace	keep quiet
pile on the agony	to intensify distress
to sugar the pill	to make an unpleasant situation less unpleasant
child's play	very easy
pound of flesh	complete payment
pull one's weight	use all one's efforts
put two and two together	to deduce something from given facts
put the wind up	to frighten
queer one's pitch	spoil one's chances beforehand
open question	debatable matter
in the red	in debt
ring a bell	remind someone about something
rise with the lark	to get up early
root and branch	every part
in the running	in with a chance of success
rush one's fences	be in too great a hurry to get results
the sands are running out	there is not too much time left
hold the scales	to be impartial
scrape through	succeed by a narrow margin
second to none	better than all others

Idiom	Meaning
set one's face against	to oppose
settle someone's hash	to spoil someone's plans
the sheet anchor	the chief support
all over the shop	everywhere
like a shot	speedily
at sixes and sevens	to be muddled
to have a skeleton in the cupboard	to have a disgrace which the family or community tries to hide
to be sold a pup	to be cheated
in the soup	in difficulty
sour grapes	to speak disparagingly of something but only because it is unattainable
call a spade a spade	to speak plainly
spick and span	neat and tidy
throw a sprat to catch a mackerel	risk a little to gain a lot
strain at a gnat and swallow a camel	object to something trivial while permitting a greater offence
stumbling-block	an obstacle
a place in the sun	a favourable position
cross swords with	to quarrel with
taken for a ride	deceived
take the rough with the smooth	able to accept both unpleasant and pleasant things
a tall story	an improbable tale
as thick as thieves	very friendly
throw dust in one's eyes	deceive
tickled to death	very amused
bide one's time	to wait patiently
pressed for time	very busy
tip the wink	to warn
long in the tooth	old
an ivory tower	a refuge from harsh realities
trump up	to state falsely
turn one's back on	to ignore deliberately
turn the tables	reverse the position
twiddle one's thumbs	to waste one's time
under one's wing	to be protected
on one's uppers	very poor

Idiom	Meaning
with velvet gloves	gently
taking a long view	planning over a period of time
give voice to	express
with one voice	unanimously
with one's back to the wall	to be desperate
wash-out	complete failure
hold water	to be true
throw cold water on	to discourage
well-to-do	fairly rich
have the whip hand	to be in a position to control
wide of the mark	inaccurate
get wind of	obtain early knowledge about something likely to happen
wink at	ignore tactfully
wring one's withers	cause distress to
within easy reach	accessible
do wonders	have remarkable successes
make short work of	finish quickly
make the best of both worlds	to satisfy two opposing demands
wrapped up in	absorbed in
the writing on the wall	give a clear warning of imminent disaster
get hold of the wrong end of the stick	to be completely wrong about something
yellow-livered	cowardly
yeoman-service	excellent work
pull yourself together	to take control of your emotions

THE ORIGINS OF OUR LANGUAGE

Pure-bred English has never existed for our language comes from a number of sources. We have borrowed extensively from other languages and from each nation that has invaded us. Thus, from the Celts we get words like *glen, knob, mug, pool* and *taper.* From the Romans who invaded in 55 B.C. we borrowed words like *mite, wine* and *wall.* The Jutes, Angles and Saxons who invaded next established their own language. We call the language they used Old English or Anglo-Saxon. Most of our everyday English words come from this source. Words like *and, find, good, under, was, well, when* and *would.* To these the coming of Christianity in A.D.597 resulted in religious-type words being added: some of these are *altar, bishop, candle, Christmas* and *disciple.*

Towards the end of the 8th century the Danish Vikings invaded England. Eventually, they began to settle here and gave our language well-known words like *call, clip, clumsy, husband, knife, outlaw* and *want.* In the 11th century, the Danes were followed by the Normans. Grammar school pupils began to be taught in Norman-French. Gradually, as the Normans became isolated from France and intermarried with the Anglo-Saxons the two languages mingled and Middle English as it is called was born. This is the language used by Geoffrey Chaucer in his "Canterbury Tales". The French connection gave our language words like *charity, comedy, humour, justice, tragedy,* and *trespass.*

The Renaissance (rebirth of learning) which came to England in the 15th and 16th centuries added Latin and ancient Greek words to the language. From Latin we derived words like *accommodate, distinguish, estimate, manufacture* and *tradition;* and from Greek, *climax, emphasis, epidemic, paragraph* and *synonym.* The use of Greek and Latin words did not end with the Renaissance for whenever a new thing or idea has been invented language experts have tended to use Latin and Greek words to explain them. In this way, for example, the modern word *television* has been derived from Greek — *tele* (from afar) and Latin — *visus* (vision).

From the middle of the 17th century, Modern English has been in use and it has developed by enlargement of vocabulary and modifications to the meaning of existing words. As well as the major linguistic accretions already mentioned, there have been dozens of minor ones. Italian culture, Dutch sea power, the industrial and scientific revolutions, the American influence in film and broadcasting, World Wars I and II, the atomic and space age and the coming of computers have all given us new words.

From Italy come, for example, the words *concerto, fresco* and *replica:* from the Dutch, the words *deck* and *yacht:* from science, words like *bacteria, oxygen, telescope* and *supersonic:* from America, those like *commuter, elevator, ban* and *gangster.* The World Wars have given us *camouflage, U-boat, airstrip, gestapo, blitz* and *sabotage,* while the atomic and space age and computers have given us words like *fall-out, sputnik, space-travel, print-out* and the *silicon chip.*

Finally, the following contains examples of borrowing from a variety of other languages.

Arabic — *algebra, caliph, coffee and cotton*
Chinese — *china, nankeen, tea*
Egyptian — *gum, gipsy, oasis, paper*
German — *meerschaum, swindle, waltz*
Hebrew — *amen, cherub, jubilee*
Hindustani — *bangle, dacoit, chutney*
Malay — *amuck, bamboo, cockatoo, orang-outang*
Mexican — *chocolate, cocoa, tomato*
North-American Indian — *moccasin, tobacco, tomahawk*
Persian — *bazaar, caravan, chess, dervish, jackal, lilac*
Peruvian — *guano, llama, pampas, puma*
Polynesia — *taboo, tattoo (skin)*
Portuguese — *apricot, cobra, dodo, emu, lingo*
Russian — *Bolshevik, mazurka, rouble, soviet, steppe*
Sanskrit — *chintz, ginger, juggernaut, pundit, rajah*
Spanish — *Armada, banana, cargo, cigar, don, quixotic*
Syria — *damask, damson, Messiah, muslin*
Tibetan — *lama, yak*
Turkish — *fey, horde, turkey*

Foreign words, and phrases

As we have seen foreign words are responsible for the derivation of many words that we now take to be English. There are also words we use which have not been absorbed into the language but which we use knowing them to be foreign. A student needs to know the most common of these as they often appear in English prose. A short list is given.

FROM FRENCH

Word or phrase	Meaning
adieu	farewell
aide-mémoire	an aid to memory
à la carte	a menu stating the price for each dish
a la mode	fashionable
amour	love
amour-propre	self-esteem
ancien régime	the old system
à propos	to the purpose
à propos des bottes	with regard to nothing in particular
arriere-pensée	a mental note
attaché	a member of the staff of a legation
au fait	well acquainted with a particular matter
au revoir	goodbye (until we meet again)
à votre santé	good health
beau monde	the people of fashion
belles-lettres	polite literature
bête-noire	a bugbear
blasé	bored
bon mot	a clever remark
bon vivant	someone fond of good living
bon voyage	wishing good luck to someone going on a journey
bric-á-brac	odds and ends
carte blanche	a free hand
cause celebre	a famous law-case
chef-d'oeuvre	a masterpiece
coup de grace	the last stroke; mercy killing
coup d'état	a change of government by force
creme de la crème	cream of the cream — the very best
cuisine	cooking
cul-de-sac	a blind alley
débris	scattered pieces
début	first appearance, especially theatrical

Word or phrase	Meaning
éclair	a type of pastry
élite	the best people
embarras de choix	embarassment of choice — too many to choose from
embarras de richesse	embarassment of riches — so much wealth that one does not know what to do with it
en bloc	in total, in bulk
encore	once more, again
en famille	at home
enfant terrible	a terrible child
en masse	all together
ennui	boredom
en rapport	in sympathy with
entre nous	between you and me, confidentially
etiquette	rules of behaviour
fait accompli	an accomplished fact
faux pas	a mistake
force majeure	superior force
habitué	a regular
hors de combat	disabled
hors-d'oeuvre	a savoury side-dish taken at the beginning of a meal
idée fixe	a fixed idea
impasse	deadlock
laisser-faire	to let alone — not to interfere
mal à propos	out of place
matinee	afternoon performance
naive	ingenuous, natural
nom de plume	a pen name
nonpareil	without equal
panache	with a flourish
par excellence	above all
parvenu	a newcomer
pied-à-terre	a temporary lodging
precis	a summary
protégé	someone under another's protection or influence
sabotage	deliberate damage (usually for political ends)

Word or phrase	Meaning
sang-froid	in cold blood
savoir-faire	tact, knowing what to do
table d'hote	a set meal served at a fixed price
tête-a-tête	a private talk
tout ensemble	all together; the general impression
voilà-tout	that is all
volte-face	a turnabout — to change one's views completely

FROM LATIN

ad hoc	for this
ad infinitum	endless
ad nauseam	never ending (sickening)
a fortiori	all the more
ante meridiem	before noon
bona fide	good faith
circa	about
compos mentis	of sound mind
contra	against
de facto	in fact
de jure	according to the law
et cetera	and the rest
et sequitur	and the following
exempli gratia	for example
ex libris	from the library (of)
ex officio	because of one's office
finis	the end
hic jacet	here lies
in camera	heard in private
inter alia	among other things
lipsus linguae (memoriae)	a slip of the tongue (memory)
locum tenens	taking the place of (someone)
mea culpa	by my own fault
modus operandi	a way of working
mutatis mutandis	with any needful change of detail
ne plus ultra	the utmost limit
nota bene	note well
opus	work

Word or phrase	Meaning
per annum	every year
per diem (mensem)	by day (by month)
post meridian/iem	afternoon
post mortem	after death
post scriptum	written afterwards
prima facie	first impression
pro patria	for one's country
pro rata	proportionately
pro tempore	for the time being
sic	thus
sine die	an unspecified date
sine qua non	an essential
sotto voce	quietly, in an undertone
status quo	to leave things as they are
stet	let it stand
ubique	everywhere
ultra vires	beyond one's power
versus	against
via media	the middle way
vice	in the place of
vice versa	conversely
viva voce	orally

Words from proper names

Some of our words owe their origin to the names of people and places. The best know of these are:

Academy   from the Greek Akademia, a grave near Athens where Pluto was a teacher.

Arcadian   from the Greek Arkadia, a mountainous, country area in the Peloponnesus.

August   the month named after the Roman Emperor Augustus.

Bayonet   the name for a dagger derived from Bayonne in France.

Bunkum   from the name of a county in North Carolina, U.S.A., where the congressman insisted on talking endless nonsense — "making a speech for Buncombe".

Bunsen burner   from Professor Bunsen of Heidelberg, Germany, the inventor.

Boycott   from the name of Captain Boycott who was sent to Coventry (completely ignored) by the Irish.

Calico   material originally from Calicut (India).

Canter   the way in which the Canterbury pilgrims rode their horses.

Champagne   wine originally distilled in the French region of that name.

Cognac   brandy originally distilled from the French Cognac district.

Copper   a metal deriving its name from the island of Cyprus in the Mediterranean.

Currant   the dried grapes used in cooking originally came from Corinth where they got their name.

Dunce   from the name of the 14th century philosopher John Duns Scotus opposed to the new learning brought by the Renaissance.

Epicure   a follower of the Greek philosopher Epicurus who taught that pleasure was supreme.

Ermine   a fur, comes from Armenia.

Grog   the nickname of Admiral Vernon who used to wear a grogram cloak, and who ordered his sailors to water their rum.

Gipsy   is derived from Egypt where they supposedly originated.

Hooligan   the name of an Irish family living in Southwark, London who were notorious for their bad behaviour.

January   from the mythical Roman God Janus who faced two ways, backward to the old year and forward to the new year.

Jovial   from the name of the planet Jupiter (Jove).

Magic   from the magi, the priests of the Persians.

Malapropism	derived from Mrs. Malaprop who was always getting her words muddled up in Sheridan's play, "The Rivals".
Macadam	from the name of the famous road-maker, J. L. McAdam.
Milliner	from the Italian town Milan famous for ribbons and gloves.
Muslin	comes from Mosul, a town on the river Tigris.
Panic	fear, supposed to have come from the noise made by Pan, the God of Shepherds.
Port	originally the name of wine coming from Oporto (Portugal).
Quixotic	from Cervantes' novel "Don Quixote".
Sandwich	comes from John Montague, the Earl of Sandwich who disliked leaving the gaming tables and had meals sent to him consisting of cold meats between slices of toast.
Sardonic	scornful, comes from a poisonous Sardinian plant.
Sherry	originally the name of wine from Xeres (Spain).
Shrapnel	comes from the name of Shrapnel, a British General.
Silhouette	from the name of a French barber who cut 'silhouettes' of his clients from paper.
Stoical	indifferent to pleasure or pain— comes from the Greek stoa, the porch in Athens where Zeno taught his pupils.
Tantalise	from the punishment of Tantalus, a king in Greek mythology who was compelled to remain thirsty although surrounded by water.
Tawdry	from St. Etheldrida the patron saint of Ely, East Anglia. Originally, 'tawdry lace' was bought at an annual fair.
Thursday	from the day of Thor, god of thunder.
Troy-weight	from weights used at the Troyes Fair (France).

Utopian	the name for an imaginary place mentioned in Sir Thomas More's novel of that name.
Vandal	the name is derived from a nation of invaders who laid waste the Roman Empire.
Volcano	from Vulcan a God whose forge was situated below Etna.

Dialect words, archaic words and americanisms

We now come to words which are not permissible in correct literary usage. The first of these are **dialect.** These are words which are used in everyday speech in certain regions of the country. In Wales, Scotland, the West Country and the North Country there are numerous dialects which are difficult for an Englishman to understand if he is a stranger. Examples are "ourn" for ours, "chider" for children (West Country) "laking" for playing (North) and in Scotland "wee" for little or "bairns" for children. In London, too, there is a cockney dialect with the added problem of rhyming slang which people find it difficult to understand — "Rosy Lea" for tea and "inky smudge" for judge.

Archaisms are words which are no longer in use and should also not be used. Examples are:

anon	later
hallow	a saint
nonce	for the nonce, i.e., for the time being
prithee	I pray thee, please
twain	two
welkin	a cloud
whilom	formerly
willy-nilly	will I, will I not
yclept	called, named
yore	year

Americanisms are words used in American-English. They have different meanings in the U.K. H. W. Horwill explains the problems of Americanisms in his book *Modern American Usage:* "Few of us, perhaps, realize what a subtle and frequent cause of misunderstanding lurks in the fact that so many familiar words are used in America with a different meaning, or at any rate with a different implication, from that which they bear in England. On both sides of the Atlantic we speak a common language, but if that common language has not always a common meaning, its employment as a means of communication is beset by many pitfalls". For example:

British	American
a flat	apartment
banknotes	bankpaper
picnic	basket lunch or dinner
pageboy	bellhop
wallet	billfold
lounge suit	business suit
sweets	candy
draughts	checkers
bank account	checking account
clothes-peg	clothes pin
small sweet cake	cookie
biscuit	cracker
pack of cards	deck of cards
ground floor	first floor
suspenders (men's)	garters
bonnet (of a car)	hood
petrol	gas
pig	hog
garden party	lawn party
timber	lumber
bookstall	news-stand
boot (of a car)	trunk
trousers	pants
handbag	purse
pavement	sidewalk
formal evening clothes	soup and fish
braces for trousers	suspenders
waistcoat	vest
shop	store
sunset	sundown
sunrise	sunup
terminus	terminal

PRACTICE QUESTIONS

1. Give adjectives from the following words:

    Academy; August; Epicure; Gargantua; Grog; Hercules; Mars; McAdam; Mercury; Pasteur; Quixote; Satan; Stentor and Utopia.

2. Explain the meaning of the following:

    (i) the great unwashed

    (ii) an itching palm

    (iii) the psychological moment

    (iv) a leading light

    (v) gilt-edged investments

    (vi) plight one's troth

    (vii) a past-master

    (viii) shipshape and Bristol fashion

    (ix) make heavy weather

    (x) cheek by jowl

3. Explain the following slang words or expressions:

(i) curtains	(vi) landslide
(ii) a doddle	(vii) let rip
(iii) fit to drop	(viii) off the record
(iv) high jinks	(ix) past it
(v) I should cocoa	(x) screwball

4. Explain the following clichés:

    (ix) another Richmond in the same field

    (ii) the apple of discord

    (iii) a boon companion

    (iv) to chop and change

    (v) a Daniel come to judgement

    (vi) dyed in the wool

(vii) the Emerald Isle

(viii) to gain ground

(ix) hands across the sea

(x) to mark time

5. Explain the following English idioms and give the literal meaning of each:

(i) an account to settle	(vi) as large as life
(ii) come to anchor	(vii) go out of one's mind
(iii) at arm's length	(viii) on the rocks
(iv) buy the moon	(ix) in the saddle
(v) knock on the head	(x) tear into ribbons (or tatters)

6. What do the following idioms mean?

    A bottleneck; green-eyed monster; a blue-pencil; a brown study; a bread-winner; bad blood; all agog; elbow-room; a grass widow.

7. Give the equivalent in English of the following words or phrases borrowed from other languages:

    Billet-doux; bonhomie; betise; bonne mouche; bon ton; chaperon; chic; comme il faut; dénouement; double entendre; doyen; ad valorem; Anno Domini; caveat emptor; cum grano salis; fidus achates; flagrante delicto; idem est; magnum opus; mirabile dictu.

8. Rewrite the following, avoiding the use of any hackneyed phrases:

    (i) After a long walk it was time that we refreshed the inner man.

    (ii) He was such a handsome fellow that he made a strong appeal to the fair sex.

    (iii) John went on his travels leaving his better half at home.

    (iv) The anecdote he told was too funny for words.

    (v) He told us that it was a consummation devoutly to be wished.

(vi) The committee was surrounded by five young hopefuls for the position.

(vii) We were left to the tender mercies of the conductor.

(viii) The ball was conspicuous by its absence.

(ix) The board of directors all feared that they might be displaced by one of the rising generation.

(x) He waited and then gave his decision at the critical time.

9. From which language are the following words derived?

Cotton; jubilee; boom; landscape; bouquet; caprice; debonair; annual; anniversary; tea; fascism; strafe.

10. The following sentences contain examples of Americanisms which are in italics. Give the British equivalent of these words:

(i) He went to the *city hall* to pay his taxes.

(ii) The scenery looked lovely in the *fall* as the leaves turned a golden colour.

(iii) The *cycler* put on his clips and rode off at full speed.

(iv) John Jones was a *drummer* for a firm of biscuit manufacturers and was good at his job.

ANSWERS TO PRACTICE QUESTIONS

ESSENTIAL SPELLING

1. Plentiful | boyish | carriage
   merrily | enjoyment | annoyance
   reliable | multiplication | variable
   victorious | sleepiness | various
   undeniable | ignominious | stickiest

2. Humorous | labourious | entrance
   wintry | carpentry | repetition
   encumbrance | disastrous | impetuosity
   tigress | humorist | curiosity

3. Advantageous | manageable | behaviour
   embraced | peaceable | lovable
   disparagement | gracious | tiresome
   arranging | couragious | pleasure
   tracing | aging | saviour

4. Confidence | disobedience | maintenance
   obedience | performance | presence
   acceptance | absence | violence
   tolerance | insurance | assistance
   impertinence | grievance |

5. Mathematics | miniature | fatigue
   development | acquaintance | spacious
   courageous | privilege | pigeon
   embarrass | dialogue | arctic
   scenery | vague | harass

6. (i) Prosecuted; (ii) prescribed; (iii) absent; (iv) aesthetic; (v) bravado; (vi) century; (vii) contagious; (viii) depreciate; (ix) disinterested, guilt; (x) draught; (xi) epitaph; (xii) famous.

7. We were forced to *wait* for Gerald and Tom who were not *due* to arrive until seven. With time hanging *heavy* on our *hands* we decided to *approach* a small *restaurant* which we *knew* was *nearby*. Brian drove his car *skilfully* and *although* there was little or no *parking* space he managed to get it *neatly* alongside the kerb and *proceeded* to lock it up *securely*. We jumped out *quickly* and *immediately* went into the cafe and ordered *buttered scones*. We had no *arguments* about *what* to

eat *because* we both *liked scones.* Once we had finished our *snack* we *received* and *paid* our bill of *fare* and went back to the *place* where we were *positive* we would *meet* our *friends.*

8. Accommodate; woollen; pavilion; emigrate; laboratory; effervesce; embarrass; fulfil; forfeit; diphthong; harass; government; parliament; calendar; Britain; benefitted; anonymous; business; guarantee; mischievous; necessary; whirring; yacht; vaccinate; umbrella; picnic; comparative; literature; Shakespeare; medicine.

DIRECT AND INDIRECT SPEECH

1. "Uncle Bob, a man called Jack Thomas phoned this evening. He says he understands that you want to sell your car and as he is moving into the area he may be interested in making an offer for it. He wants to know if it is convenient for him to come to see you next Thursday. Would you please phone Burslem 58321 to let him know if it is alright?"

2. The agitated Mr. Winkle asked Mary whether Miss Allen was in the garden now. The pretty housemaid replied she did not know and that the best thing to be done would be for Mr. Weller to give him a hoist up into the tree and perhaps Mr. Pickwick would have the goodness to see that nobody came up the lane while she watched the other end of the garden. She then asked what that light was. Mr. Pickwick then turned hastily and expressing sorrow said that he did not mean to have done that. Sam then asked him to shut the lantern up. Pickwick remarked that it was the most extraordinary lantern he had ever met with in all his life and that he had never seen such a powerful reflection.

3. His speech has become thick and indistinct, Jasper, quiet and self-possessed, looks to Neville, as if expecting his answer or comment. When Neville speaks his speech is also thick and indistinct.

"It might have been better for Mr. Drood to have known some hardships," he says, defiantly.

"Pray," retorts Edwin, turning merely his eyes in that direction, "pray why might it have been better for Mr. Drood to have known some hardships?"

"Ay," Jasper assents, with an air of interest; "let us know why?"

"Because they might have made him more sensible," says Neville, "of good fortune that is not by any means necessarily the result of his own merits."

Mr. Jasper quickly looks to his nephew for his rejoinder.

"Have you known hardships, may I ask?" says Edwin Drood,

sitting upright.
>
> Mr. Jasper quickly looks to the other for his retort.
>
> "I have."

FIGURES OF SPEECH AND LITERARY APPRECIATION

1.   At the Setting of the Sun

  (i) The story is about a young man mistakenly shooting his sweetheart thinking she was a wild bird (a swan). She does not mind being in paradise thus she is happy although dead.

  (ii) The last verse expresses the bitter loneliness of the young man left without his sweetheart. He cannot love anyone else.

  (iii) The lesson to be learnt is take care when out shooting at dusk — you may kill someone.

  (iv) Similies are used in this stanza. In the second line the girl is compared with a bird in its nest and the heaviness of the burden he is carrying is expressed by the lead image in line 3. Heaviness of his heart is compared with the heaviness of lead.

  (v) She comes back from death as a ghost to comfort him.

  (vi) His own death because then he can be with his beloved again. The word *rising* is significant because it stresses the newness of the life he is to lead again with his beloved. The word *setting* repeated emphasizes the end of things for him and there is an implied image between the end of a day and the end of his life when he killed her.

2.   (a) Personification — moon compared to human walking over the sky in silver coloured shoes.

  (b) Apostrophe.

  (c) Personification — comparison between a book and a preserved human body writing for eternal life.

  (d) Metaphor — library compared with a tree.

  (e) Apostrophe.

  (f) Apostrophe.

  (g) Similes — love compared with a red rose and a tuneful song.

  (h) Metonymy — Sceptre and crown — kings and queens — Scythe and spade — farm labourers and peasants.

  (i) Hyperbole.

(j) Apostrophe.

(k) Apostrophe.

(l) Assonance.

(m) Alliteration.

(n) Balanced antithesis.

(o) Onomatopeoia.

3. Assonance.

4. (i) He lost all his money on the horses and it was a *black* day for him.

(ii) Although he thought he knew the girl she gave him the *cold* shoulder ignoring him completely.

(iii) The *root* cause of the economic problems of this country is inflation.

(iv) The *key* player in the side plays at inside forward.

(v) The *door* to success opens with a good education.

5. (i) To live from hand to mouth — *to live in great poverty;*

(ii) to turn turtle — *to capsize;*

(iii) to rush from pillar to post — *to move from place to place in panic;*

(iv) to set sail — *to start (a voyage);*

(v) by hook or by crook — *by fair means or foul;*

(vi) to turn in — *to go to bed;*

(vii) to stick to one's guns — *to refuse to change one's views;*

(viii) to be run down — *to be overtired and feeling ill;*

(ix) to pull the wool over someone's eyes — *to hide the truth from someone;*

(x) to pull one's socks up — *to make a greater effort;*

(xi) to pass out — *to faint;*

(xii) to make hay while the sun shines — *to take one's opportunity;*

(xiii) to make a mountain out of a molehill — *to exaggerate the importance of something;*

(xiv) to make a clean breast of something — *to confess fully to something;*

(xv) to keep something up one's sleeve — *to keep something secret.*

6. (i) As sound as a *bell;*
 (ii) as bold as *brass;*
 (iii) as dull as *ditchwater;*
 (iv) as safe as *houses;*
 (v) as fit as a *fiddle;*
 (vi) as dead as a *doornail*
   (or *mutton*);
 (vii) as *black* as ink;
 (viii) as *cool* as a cucumber;
 (ix) as *mad* as a hatter;
 (x) as *yellow* as saffron;
 (xi) as *pleased* as punch;
 (xii) as *fast* as lightning.

7. (i) A shark — *we do not trust him;*

   (ii) a monkey — *he is mischevious;*

   (iii) a worm — *he does not stand up for his rights;*

   (iv) a snake — *same as (i) above;*

   (v) a mouse — *he is timid.*

LETTER WRITING

Descriptions — simple objects

(i) Oxygen:	a gas which sustains both life and combustion.
(ii) a visa:	an official document issued by a particular country giving permission for foreigners to travel within its borders.
(ii) a policeman:	an official whose main purpose is to administer and uphold the law.
(iv) a waiter:	a worker who specialises in serving food and meals to people in a restaurant.
(v) flour:	finely ground grain used for making bread and cakes.
(vi) a roof:	the uppermost surface of a building or vehicle.
(vii) a garden spade:	a tool used for digging or weeding which has a wooden handle and a broad, metal blade (note these may be small for weeding or large for digging).
(viii) porridge:	a breakfast cereal made from oats.
(ix) hydrogen:	a gas which is the lightest known to man.
(x) an electric torch:	a device with a bulb and a battery used as a form of lighting.

VOCABULARY WORK

1.   (i) Have you *brought* the records?

    (ii) I have to go *now*.

    (iii) They have just *bought* a house.

    (iv) I wonder when we shall *arrive* home?

    (v) "*Fetch* your mackintosh, it's raining," he said.

2.   (i) She is such a *pleasant* lady.

    (ii) You are in a *difficult* predicament now.

    (iii) It is *pleasant* and cool in here.

    (iv) That is an *impertinent* remark to make.

    (v) The grandfather was a *charming* old man.

3.   (i) We have eaten *too much* today.

    (ii) The crooner sang a *melodious* song.

    (iii) Don't fret yourself, I shall be alright.

    (iv) We have had an *enjoyable* time today.

    (v) Don't you agree with me? (Answer) *Yes,* certainly.

4.   (i) Addicted — habitual craving for
      devoted — dedicated

    (ii) adverse — hostile
      averse — dislike

    (ii) artful — wily, cunning
      artless — simple, natural, ingenuous

    (iv) careless — negligent, inaccurate
      carefree — without worry

    (v) character — person's idiosyncracies or traits
      reputation — opinion of a person's character

    (vi) classic — excellent, of the highest class
      classics — Latin and Greek languages
      classical — Latin and Greek art and literature and the music
               of the great composers.

    (vii) considerable — important (persons), a great many (things)
      considerate — thoughtful, kind

(viii) contagious — disease spread by physical contact
contiguous — adjoining

(ix) credible — can be believed
creditable — reputable, bringing credit to

(x) deprecate — to express disapproval of
depreciate — to lessen the value of

(xi) discomfit — to perplex, throw into confusion, to disconcert
discomfort — to make someone physically uncomfortable
or mentally uneasy

(xii) distinct — clear, obvious
distinctive — characteristic

(xiii) eatable — food that can be eaten, satisfactory food
edible — capable of being prepared as food (not poisonous)

(xiv) effective — capable of bringing (something) about
efficient — giving satisfactory results
efficacious — producing the desired result (used only with
such things as remedies and medicines)

(xv) entrant — a person who has recently joined (e.g., a school
or club)
entry — a document or a name on a list

(xvi) extended — lengthy, prolonged
extensive — huge, large, detailed

(xvii) favourable — suitable, approved
favourite — liked, preferred

(xviii) glance — look at briefly
glimpse — catch sight of briefly

(xix) honorary — something given as an honour, not paid
honourable — worthy of honour

(xx) imaginary — normal; existing in the imagination
imaginative — having an inventive mind

5. (i) Infer — draw a conclusion; read a meaning into
imply — to suggest (without stating)

(ii) ingenious — skilful, clever
ingenuous — frank, sincere

(iii) Jacobean — pertaining to James I and his reign
Jacobite — supporters of the exiled Stuart kings, descendants
of James II

(iv) laudable — deserving praise
laudatory — giving praise

   (v) masterful — assertive, strong-willed
       masterly — extremely skilful

  (vi) perceive — become aware of
       conceive — imagine, devise, to become pregnant

 (vii) pitiable — wretched
       pitiful — evoking pity

(viii) potent — powerful, strong
       potential — possible

  (ix) relative — related, relating specifically to one thing
       relevant — having a bearing on some matter

   (x) sensual — concerned with the senses and not the mind
                 (used in a deprecatory way)
       sensuous — affecting the senses

  (xi) specially — for this purpose only
       especially — to a degree beyond all others

 (xii) sty — the place where a pig is kept
       stye — painful inflammation of part of the eye

(xiii) swat — to kill a fly
       swot — to study hard for an examination (colloquialism)

 (xiv) titillate — to excite or stimulate the mind or senses
       titivate — to smarten up, to make up

  (xv) tortious — a tort (in law, a civil wrong)
       tortuous — winding, involved
       torturous — inflicting pain or torture

 (xvi) triumphant — victorious
       triumphal — celebrating success or victory

(xvii) vicious — immoral, bad, depraved
       viscous — thick, syrup-like consistency

(xviii) wrapped — enclosed by some kind of fabric or material
       rapt — absorbed in

 (xix) candid — open, honest
       candied — preserved in sugar

  (xx) introvert — describes a person who is withdrawn
       extrovert — describes a person who is vivacious

   (i) Banal   (ii) conjugal
 (iii) topical   (iv) ephemeral
   (v) bilingual   (vi) habitual
 (vii) perennial   (vii) diurnal
  (ix) nocturnal   (x) eternal

(xi) paternal
(xii) spiritual
(xiii) corporal
(xiv) vernal
(xv) continual
(xvi) biennial
(xvii) bridal
(xviii) economical
(xix) inimical
(xx) conical
(xxi) identical
(xxii) fundamental
(xxiii) elemental
(xxiv) detrimental
(xxv) Oriental (Occidental

7.
Down	small feathers; hill; direction; to knock down
canon	a Church rank; a rule of law
bill	an account rendered; beak of a bird
corn	grain; callous on the foot
charger	large, flat dish; officer's horse
leaves	departs; more than one leaf

8.
(i) Polygon
(ii) pentagon
(iii) microscope
(iv) thermometer
(v) barometer
(vi) X-ray
(vii) spirit-level
(vii) plumb-line
(ix) dynamo
(x) turbine
(xi) theodolite
(xii) megaphone
(xiii) radio
(xiv) compass
(xv) magneto

9. (i) We are not *allowed* to speak during a church sermon.

(ii) He will give us no *peace* until we give him another *piece* of apple tart.

(iii) The conductor paid us some very pretty *compliments* after our performance.

(iv) Jane did not *practise* the piano very long this morning.

(v) Before us, we saw a very *precipitous* path.

10. (i) John is a most *annoying* person.

(ii) We noticed a very strange-looking *person* approaching our car.

(iii) The popular music was so loud that it *almost* raised the roof.

(iv) Harry is a friend of *both* Tom and Joe.

(v) Mary told us what *happened* at the meeting.

11.   (i) The girl said she liked the present as well as the other.

    (ii) Pigeons abound in these islands.

    (iii) We shall be delighted to co-operate with you.

    (iv) A unique feature of the variety programme is the few people used.

    (v) He recovered rapidly from his illness.

    (vi) The two 'buses collided at great speed.

    (vii) The orchestra was inaudible.

    (viii) I was seated alone in the corner.

    (ix) The general resigned.

    (x) If you agree, we will send it at once.

STYLES OF WRITING AND LANGUAGE

1.   Academic; augustinian; epicurean; gargantuan; groggy; herculean; martian; macadamize; mercurial; pasturization; quixotic; satanic; stentorian and utopian.

2.   (i) The working classes

    (ii) greed for money

    (iii) at the critical time

    (iv) a prominent person

    (v) putting money into something where there is no risk of losing the capital

    (vi) make a formal promise to marry

    (vii) an expert

    (viii) tidy and in good order

    (ix) make difficulties where few exist

    (x) very near; close together

3.   (i) The end

    (ii) a very simple piece of work or undertaking

    (iii) exhausted

    (iv) spirited entertainment

    (v) I do not worry

    (vi) sweeping and sensational charge

(vii) allow to proceed without hindrance

(viii) for private information and not for publication

(ix) too old

(x) an eccentric person

4. (i) Someone else engaged in the same work or enterprise

(ii) a source of contention

(iii) a pleasant, merry friend

(iv) to change constantly

(v) an exemplary arbitrator or judge

(vi) completely, out and out

(vii) Ireland

(viii) to progress

(ix) friendship with those abroad

(x) to make no progress

5. (i) Metaphorical — a grudge or grievance to avenge.
    Literal — a debt to pay.

(ii) Metaphorical — to stop.
    Literal — a ship lowers her anchor and stops moving.

(iii) Metaphorical — formal and unfriendly.
    Literal — the length of an extended arm.

(iv) Metaphorical — to take a futile action.
    Literal — to howl like an animal at the moon.

(v) Metaphorical — destroy.
    Literal — kill.

(vi) Metaphorical — prominent.
    Literal — in person.

(vii) Metaphorical — become irritated or confused.
    Literal — to go insane.

(viii) Metaphorical — in financial or other trouble.
    Literal — shipwrecked.

(ix) Metaphorical — in control of any enterprise.
    Literal — riding a horse.

(x) Metaphorical — destroy (e.g. someone's views or arguments).
    Literal — tear roughly into small pieces.

6.   A bottleneck — refers to a passage which suddenly becomes narrow like the neck of a bottle, causing delay. Thus, it refers to anything causing delay.
Green-eyed monster — jealousy.
A blue-pencil — to censor a piece of writing.
A brown study — absorbed in serious thought.
A bread-winner — a person whose earnings support a family.
Bad blood — antagonism.
All agog — in a state of excitement.
A grass-widow — a woman whose husband is away for long periods.

7.   Billet-doux — a love letter; bonhomie — good nature; betise — a silly action;
bonne mouche — a tasty morsel;
bon ton — good taste;
chaperon — a married or elderly female who accompanies a girl on social occasions;
chic — fashionable, stylish;
comme il faut — as it should be;
dénouement — the unravelling (especially of a plot in a film or play);
double entendre — a double meaning;
doyen — senior or oldest member;
ad valorem — according to value;
Anno Domini — in the year of our Lord;
caveat emptor — let the buyer beware;
cum grano salis — with a grain of salt;
fidus Achates — a faithful follower;
flagrante delicto — in the act;
idem est — that is;
magnum opus — great work;
mirabile dictu — wonderful to relate.

8.   (i) After a long walk it was time that we *ate*.

  (ii) He was such a handsome fellow that he made a strong appeal to the *women*.

  (iii) John went on his travels leaving his *wife* at home.

  (iv) The anecdote he told was *hilarious*.

  (v) He told us that it was *an end that was desirable*.

  (vi) The committee was surrounded by five *potential candidates* for the position.

  (vii) We were left *in the charge* of the conductor.

  (viii) The ball was *missing*.

(ix) The board of directors all feared that they might be displaced by one of the *younger people.*

(x) He waited and then gave his decision at the *psychological moment.*

9.　　　Cotton — Arabic; jubilee — Hebrew; boom — Dutch; landscape — Dutch; bouquet — French; caprice — French; debonair — French; annual — Latin; anniversary — Latin; tea — China; fascism — Italian; strafe — German.

10.　(i) City hall — town hall;

　(ii) fall — autumn;

　(iii) cycler — cyclist;

　(iv) drummer — representative, commercial traveller.